The FEMINIST TAKEOVER

BETTY STEELE · The FEMINIST TakeOver

Patriarchy
to Matriarchy
in Two
Decades

 Simon & Pierre
Toronto, Canada

We would like to express our gratitude to the Canada Council and the Ontario Arts Council for their support.
    Marian M. Wilson, Publisher

Canadian Cataloguing in Publication Data

Steele, Betty,
        The feminist takeover

Includes bibliographical references.
ISBN 0-88924-236-4

            Feminism. 2. Women - Canada - Social conditions
            Canada - Social conditions. I. Title.

HQ1154.S74 1991   305.42C91 094905-0

First published in 1987 by Tercet, Toronto, Canada

Text Design: Eskins Stevens Design, Toronto, Canada
Typesetting: Fleet Typographers Limited /
Printed in Canada by John Deyell Company

Order from
Simon & Pierre Publishing Company Limited /
Les Éditions Simon & Pierre Ltée
P.O. Box 280 Adelaide Street Postal Station
Toronto, Ontario, Canada M5C 2J4

To My Husband
Gordon Gilmour Steele, M.COM.,
whose research expertise
made this book possible

CONTENTS

PREFACE

By the late Seventies, I became convinced that the quality of life in Canada was deteriorating, and I began to trace many problems in our society back to the new ideology of the Women's Liberation Movement. As a beleaguered housewife continuously downgraded in the media, increasingly belittled in society generally as a result of such media influence, and reduced to a Ms. on all my mail against my wishes, I came to believe that I was being manipulated — as in a dictatorship.

As a journalist (formerly a news editor of *Marketing*, an editor on *New World*, and a freelance writer for radio, magazines, and newspapers) I decided to develop a thesis and write a book. As a trained observer and voracious reader accustomed to delving into international libraries, such as the Colindale in London, England, where the first issues of *The Times* are stored, and where I found my background historical material, I have necessarily adopted a journalist's approach to the task.

This book attempts to examine carefully all the ramifications of the Women's Liberation Movement, the movement that has grown into a revolution of gigantic proportions, changing the lives of every man, woman, and child on the continent. It exposes the movement's roots and dynamics, and attempts to gauge the end results. It demands at least a hearing, above the din of twenty years of feminist propaganda.

INTRODUCTION

George Gallup III, president of the Gallup Poll, the authoritative organization that has surveyed and reported weekly on political, social, and economic issues in North America during the past forty years, spoke to the prestigious Empire Club in Toronto, in the spring of 1985, of the "monumental political, social and economic impulses that are carrying us relentlessly toward a rendezvous with the future." He urgently warned that "we [must] make the attempt to identify these forces, because if swift, forceful steps aren't taken to defuse the political and social time bombs facing us, we may well find ourselves on a track that could lead to the possible destruction of civilization as we know it."[1]

William Reich, a Yale Professor of Law, attempted to draw an optimistic blueprint for a new world and a new culture in his book, *The Greening of America*. But thirty American critics, ranging from the editors of *Fortune* magazine to Herbert Marcuse, came to the conclusion in *The Con III Controversy*, that, in Herbert Marcuse's words, Reich's precepts were simply "sentimental sublimation," and that goals "cannot be attained by an ostrich policy."[2]

"So many people are so desperate now," Peter Marin wrote, that

> they will embrace the book simply because it allows them to evade the awful truths about where we are, how far and deep we have to go . . . we will forget what is actually missing here, and what *is* happening, and how men (and women) really live and thrive, and what we still owe one another and the young. . . .[3]

1

"We would do well to ask who the wounded may be,"[4] suggested psychologist Nancy R. McWilliams.

Anthropologist Margaret Mead, a former Women's Liberation proponent, wrote:

> Families are in trouble everywhere in a world in which change... kinds of change that in many cases we ourselves proudly initiated... has been massive and rapid, and innovations have proliferated with only the most superficial concern for their effect on human lives.

She also warned, "At a turning point... it becomes crucial to redefine what we most value and where we are headed."[5]

Women have certainly initiated all the social changes in the Women's Liberation Movement, which are leading to a matriarchy. They have not heeded the advice of Roland Barthes, who cautioned women against backing themselves into a *gynaeceum*, in his famous *Mythologies*. He wrote: "Women, be therefore courageous, free; play at being men; but never get far from them; compensate for your books [works] by your children.... Let us tie the adventure of art to the strong pillars of the home...."[6]

While men and children may seem particularly disadvantaged in a matriarchy, women may be in still greater trouble, in their determination to espouse Simone de Beauvoir's philosophy that designated human biology simply as a "female trap"[7] from which modern women may now free themselves. They are in danger of becoming "split personalities."

Stephen Strauss, in a major article in *The Globe and Mail*, in the spring of 1985, considered "the fractured humanity of women."[8]

C.G. Jung, the philosopher, had already analyzed "split personalities." He wrote:

> Separation from his instinctual nature inevitably

plunges civilized man [woman] into the conflict between conscious and unconscious, spirit and nature, knowledge and faith, a split that becomes pathological the moment his consciousness is no longer able to neglect or suppress his instinctual side. The accumulation of individuals who have got into this critical state starts off a mass movement purporting to be the champion of the suppressed.[9]

Was this the root of the Women's Liberation Movement? Has the Movement reached its zenith in a matriarchy? Or, are we still plunging, like the lemmings, into a darker sea?

1
Patriarchy to Matriarchy

If we face the fact that we are moving rapidly into a full-fledged matriarchy, we may be able to cut through the current confusion and lack of direction in our society to adjust more comfortably to the myriad changes brought about by the Women's Liberation Movement. We seem to be drifting, rudderless, some of us partially paralyzed as we cling forlornly to traditional tenets, while others are estranged and living recklessly in a completely different world, only two decades in the making. In two decades, every aspect of society has been altered irrevocably; few scholars would deny that the swift and far-reaching effects of the Women's Liberation Movement on this continent are unparallelled in the history of any continent.

While psychiatrists, psychologists, sociologists, and anthropologists throughout the United States and Canada are studying the effects, and attempting to cope with the results, they have yet to come up with any satisfactory guidelines to lead us through this great transitional period in our history. So far, they have only been warning us of new dangers — with the radical leadership becoming more radical, and the domination, oppression, and injustices that the feminists believed they recognized in a former patriarchy, being repeated in a matriarchy by a reversal of roles.

It is astonishing that the dangers are seen to be looming the largest in Canada. The thrusts of the feminist revolution in the United States and Canada have been so interwoven as to be indistinguishable, and have usually been the subject of joint studies — until the mid-Eighties. At this juncture, there is an apparent receding of the tide, and efforts to find a new balance are made throughout the United States, but not in Canada, where new strength and an increasing momentum are seen in federal and provincial legislation.

Canadian feminists exult in the fact that the Canadian Women's Liberation Movement has now forged significantly ahead of the American Women's Liberation Movement, although they concede that it was the American leaders who paved the way. Betty Friedan's book, *The Feminine Mystique*, published in 1963, certainly launched the revolutionary movement. It was Betty Friedan who founded NOW, the National Organization of Women in the United States, which successfully fought to entrench the movement's principles. Gloria Steinem, editor of the mass-circulation feminist magazine, *Ms.*; Kate Millett, the powerful lesbian feminist writer and speaker; and Bella Abzug, nicknamed "battling Bella," who battled the United States House of Representatives for six years, all inspired our own brilliant protagonists in the early years of the Canadian Movement, yet have been unable to attain comparable American legislation.

American feminist leaders in the Eighties now study the tactics of Canadian feminist leaders, such as Doris Anderson, who is the acknowledged "mother" of the Canadian Movement, and editor from 1958 to 1977 of the beloved women's magazine and home-making manual, *Chatelaine,* which has become a source of feminist ideology. Outstanding feminist influence in Canada has been wielded by Judy Erola, the former federal Liberal Cabinet Minister Responsible for the Status of Women; Lynda Hurst, strident daily columnist for *The Toronto Star*; and Chaviva Hosek, a University of Toronto English professor and president of NAC, the National Action Committee on the Status of Women, who organized the televised Women's Debate during the 1984 Canadian federal election campaign, in which all three party leaders would be reduced to "grovelling." Always supported by their publicly funded lobby groups, Canadian feminists have been able to accomplish what their American counterparts still dream of — legislation that may ensure a matriarchy.

There were feminist celebrations all over Canada, and messages of congratulation from American feminists, including Betty Friedan, when Section 15 of the Canadian Charter of Rights and Freedoms became law on April 17, 1985. Now enshrined in our Constitution, it bans discrimination on the basis of race, national or ethnic origin, colour, religion, sex, age, or mental or physical disability. However, it is the additional, subsection (2) clause, usually omitted in media reports, that is the key to the reversal in power. It states that discrimination is permissible if it is in a program designed to help the disadvantaged.

There are hundreds of women in every province now poised to prove that they are disadvantaged, while the federal and provincial legislatures have all set in motion affirmative action programs, with enormous federal and provincial funding designated to support them in the courts. For example, in Ontario in July 1985, David Peterson, within his first few days in office as the new Liberal premier, announced that his government would immediately set up a $1 million fund to support court cases based on the Women's Rights guarantees in the Charter, and that the new government would initiate further "unique programs to deal with unique needs" of women.[1]

The "unique needs" of women had also been served when the federal government appointed a major Royal Commission to study equal employment opportunities, and pay equity problems, *a Royal Commission consisting of one powerful feminist voice*, that of Ontario Provincial Court judge Rosalie Abella. Many of the 117 recommendations in her subsequent report will be drafted into permanent legislation according to federal Cabinet promises.

In the United States, President Ronald Reagan, discussing similar problems in an address to the nation, stated:

> Minorities and women can't break free if government destroys their earning power with protectionist measures that raise prices and eventually cripple the job market and our economy as well...and workers searching for jobs can't break free if government upsets the marketplace with hare-brained ideas like federally mandated comparable worth, a proposal that would take salary decisions out of the hands of employers and employees and give government the power to determine what a fair salary is.[2]

While the United States Chamber of Commerce has consistently supported the President with influential lobbying campaigns against the "derogation of free markets," no such opposition has ever been allowed to develop in Canada.

I heard one American feminist remark that Canadian men seemed, "marvelously acquiescent and conciliatory — unlike many American men. Where is there any resistance to feminist programs in Canada?" She added ruefully, "In many of our States, we will be fighting for ERA, our Equal Rights Amendment, and comparable legislation all the way to our graves." Betty Friedan told me personally, in February 1985, that it would probably take American feminists "until the year 2000" to achieve the ERA goals.

It is true that there are many "disadvantaged" men on this side of the border who are simply "lying down and playing dead." Some observers believe that this is the result of a peculiarly Canadian naiveté and innate sense of justice, combined with an overwhelming guilt complex.

Canadian feminists have ultimately been successful in convincing men and women alike of the immeasurable evils of patriarchy in the past — the domination, the oppression, and the injustices. Indifferent to female chauvinism, men are docilely retiring from every area of society, giving way to all feminist demands, in compulsive efforts to atone for the past.

The momentum of the Women's Liberation Movement in Canada never flags, but accelerates with the founding of every new women's group and women's courses in our universities, encouraged and applauded daily in all media — where women are often seen to be already in control. New government offices, commissions, and committees dealing with women's affairs blossom daily, in Ottawa and throughout the provinces. The amount of money being spent on women's concerns, exclusively, by our various governments must surely soon be calculated.

The federal government's $2.3 million annual budget for the Canadian Advisory Council on the Status of Women, comprising thirty members, is only a base sum. The National Action Committee on the Status of Women, the country's largest feminist lobby group, receives $300,000 from the Secretary of State; the Congress of Learning Opportunities for Women, $189,000; the Canadian Research Institute for the Advancement of

Women, $295,000; the National Association of Women and Law, (NAWL), $100,000; the Canadian Association for the Advancement of Women and Sport, $100,000.

The federal list is interminable, and yet the ink was barely dry on Walter McLean's appointment by Prime Minister Mulroney as Cabinet Minister Responsible for Women's Affairs, when he announced increased funding for women's groups; improved communications with women's groups; increased commitment to Equal Pay for Work of Equal Value, beginning in the federal departments; and job retraining programs to help women cope with technological change.[3]

A 32-page feminist pamphlet, entitled *The Treatment of the Sexes in Research*, that attempted to prove anti-female, sexist bias in academic research, and warned Canadian researchers against falling into foolish and erroneous sexual assumptions in their research, was produced by the Social Sciences and Humanities Research Council, a Council costing the federal government $62.8 million a year.

As more and more mothers enter the labour market — 45 per cent of them with children under the age of three and 52 per cent of them with children under the age of six are now working outside the home — the cost of day care has already risen astronomically. In the fiscal year 1984-85, the federal government spent $75 million on day care, sharing this amount with the provinces under the Canada Assistance Plan. This does not include the revenue dollars lost in income tax credits, such as the Child Care Expense Deduction, nor does it take into account the amount the provinces spend separately, which is estimated to average considerably above that in the federal budget. In 1985, Ontario established 7,500 new subsidized day care spaces at a cost of $30 million, bringing its total number of spaces available to more than 100,000. Still, universal day care, a priority feminist issue throughout the provinces, could cost the federal government more than $40 billion a year, according to Michael Krashinsky, an economist at the University of Toronto.[4]

Provincial funding for feminist causes appears inexhaustible. Although Dennis Timbrell had the portfolio for Women's Affairs for only the few short months that Frank Miller's Conservative government held power in Ontario in 1985, he and his 60-member Women's Directorate successfully pushed women's programs to the forefront of the government agenda. Ironically, the more extravagant promises of the Liberals and New Democrats to further feminist causes were certainly a factor in bringing down the Conservative government in that province, and it appears that the Liberal government is following through on those promises.

In Ontario, the Women's Directorate has an $8 million budget, and there are affirmative action managers appointed in every ministry, with a mandate to encourage women to move quickly into executive positions. Every ministry has a budget for its own affirmative action co-ordinators, with funds provided for the creation of 1,500 "bridging" positions, that will enable women to move ahead of men into the managerial jobs, rapidly increasing their representation in administration. These "bridging" positions, for which women's aptitudes are tested in rotation, are the stepping stones into all the non-traditional female jobs, such as that of a systems analyst, who may earn more than $40,000 a year in the Ministry of Revenue. This Ministry is already reported to be 41 per cent female.[5] Other provinces are copying this highly successful program. There is also the Ontario Status of Women Council with $267,800 in funding, although this is considered minimal in comparison with Quebec, a province spending $2 million annually for its Status of Women Council.

As governments pour more and more money into women's issues, the private sector is threatened and prodded to follow suit. Major banks have been among the first to comply with feminist demands for special programs and privileges. The Bank of Montreal, in its first Quarterly Report for 1985, showed that the proportion of management positions "held by women had risen to 42 per cent," while the Chairman, W.D. Mulholland, stated in a letter: "I feel confident you will see much further evidence of our desire to enhance the prospects for female staff members. The opportunity is there for women to move into the highest ranks."[6]

Then there are the private foundations, such as the anonymous one in the West that offers $760,000 to finance women in each of the Ph.D. programs of Management and Business Administration at the Universities of Alberta and British Columbia. Ten women will be accorded a special welcome and will undoubtedly receive special treatment at each university for three years, with two or three women added every year to the programs — programs that are designed to guarantee university postings, or put them securely in the top business administrative echelons across the country. There are no such programs advertised for young men.

With such encouragement, approbation, and funding, there are now no limits in the Women's Liberation Movement in Canada, as women outstrip men in opportunities and advancement in every public area of contemporary society, as well as in dictating personal relationships.

Canadian feminists, having successfully transformed our society into a matriarchy, may no longer feel the need to be segregated off into the warring women's councils and groups, and may even be willing to release some of the billions of dollars presently supporting their particular principles, their thousands of programs — billions of dollars that could then be funnelled back to address concerns and causes common to men and women, such as the federal deficit. (It is considered highly improbable that there will ever be any men's groups demanding funding to examine or change in any way their imagined or very real disadvantaged positions in a matriarchy.)

2
Hate and Vengeance in the Women's Liberation Movement

> Women must achieve equality with men. But who wants equality with animals. I don't wish to be his equal. I'm already better than he is....

Newspapers blazoned this sentiment across Canada, quoting from *HERizons*, a national feminist magazine, published in Winnipeg and partially funded by our federal agencies.

In any revolution, "hate" and "vengeance" inevitably become key elements, but they were obviously the initial characteristics of the Women's Liberation Movement in the United States and Canada, and have continued to provide the refueling.

Furthermore, I believe that "hatred" of men and "vengeance" with all its ramifications, have been the most evil and unjustified aspects of the Women's Liberation Movement. As such, they must be addressed as an urgent primary consideration, and somehow dissipated, if we would move more easily through this crucial historical period of transition. "Hate" and "vengeance" must not persist as the grim driving force in feminist agendas, obscuring truth and overshadowing our future directions.

The Hate Propaganda Act was enacted in 1971, to govern the "irrational, and malicious abuse of certain identifiable groups," or an attack on such groups in "abusive, insulting, scurrilous and false terms." It might have ensured legal action to control the venomous power that was unleashed in thousands of feminist speeches and articles, that endeavoured to establish the sins, the evil, and the guilt in men in a patriarchy.

With little warning, men had suddenly been charged and condemned, without trial or any opportunity of defence, as the "oppressors" of women, with all women having been subjected to unspeakable injustices. Subsequently, modern North American men would be saddled with the guilt of the men of all the ages, including their fathers and forefathers. Yet it can be demonstrated historically that the evils of patriarchy were seldom conceived by chauvinistic design.

In the United States in the Sixties, branches of SCUM — the Society for Cutting Up Men — were organized by American feminists from coast to coast, with widely distributed manifestoes declaring their radical principles.[1]

In Canada, the Canadian Women's Liberation Movement was said to consolidate at a conference of anti-war activists in Montreal in 1969, when strident feminists forced the focus of the agenda to be redirected toward feminist concerns. Naomi Wall, discussing the impact, wrote:

> I learned, at that conference, that women all across Canada had been cursing and caucusing and giving voice to their oppression within their new left organizations for many, many months. . . . Every woman's experience was rooted in a system that

depended for its survival on the exploitation of women — as homemakers, as sex objects, as submissive and dependent pillars of the family.... [The] very personal sense of rage we felt as girls — and then as women — was allowed to surface and find expression in the atmosphere of sisterhood provided by consciousness-raising groups. [2]

"Sisterhood" — shutting out men — developed into a menacing theme of the Women's Liberation Movement, immediately dividing the sexes into two warring camps, a development that even prominent feminists would deplore.

Betty Friedan demonstrated her concern over the burgeoning "hate" when she drafted *The Statement of Purpose of NOW* (the American National Organization of Women). The original document set forth its principles clearly: "Full equality for women, in truly equal partnership with men...in office, classroom, government and church...in marriage and the family," but it also forswore "enmity to men." NOW's executive must have signed that document, but apparently it was a hollow gesture, as the "enmity to men" would soon accelerate on both sides of the border. [3]

Bonnie Kreps, a former *Chatelaine* columnist, and a founder in 1969 of the Toronto New Feminists, one of the first and most influential of the radical feminist groups in Canada, was also strongly opposed to the smoldering "hate" and "vengeance" in the Movement. She explained:

In its sickest version, it was "I'm more radical than you because I hate men more." I was considered a liberal because I refused to accept that half the human race was incorrigibly bad.... I made an impassioned plea against rage and hatred and over-commitment to the Cause.

(In seeming frustration, Bonnie Kreps resigned from the

group, retiring to a 17-year-old marriage and mother-hood. In her writings today she is still seeking greater balance in this transitional period of history.)[4]

Doris Lessing, the renowned 65-year-old British writer, sometimes called an anti-feminist, may have been speaking for many North American women in 1984, when she told a Toronto interviewer, "From the start, I've disliked the Women's Movement shutting out men. . . . I think the Movement should have been differently structured, with men as allies and not as enemies. . . the suffragettes had a great many men as allies."[5]

However, in the modern Women's Liberation Move-ment, an age-old war tactic, *divide and conquer*, would prove successful, as the avalanche of condemnation of men and the accompanying "hate" and "vengeance" finally reached into every hamlet and home across the continent — questioning and usually rocking the foundations of every human relationship. Women would be recruited to the Cause, soon convinced of their wretched state of sub-jugation to a monstrous male "oppressor" and to the chains of childbirth.

Simone de Beauvoir had already designated pregnancy as "the female trap," but now thousands of feminist books and articles would carry that message. The Ameri-can feminist writer, Shulamith Firestone, was demand-ing "the freeing of women from the tyranny of their biology by any means available. . . Childbearing could be taken over by technology. . . ."[6] In Canada, women would be led from their husbands and homes by such speeches as that of New Feminist Dorothy Curzon, who stated: "Women who don't work are cop-outs, sitting back and watching the world go by. They live a completely unfulfilled and wasteful life."[7]

FORGING THE NEW ATTITUDES

"Liberation" then became the battle-cry, liberation from

a stifling marriage, motherhood, and homemaking, in which women were seen to have lost all physical, economic, and psychological freedom. Women across the continent who had been comfortable and satisfied with their traditional primary roles in homemaking and motherhood became convinced by the feminists that they were indeed mired in a backwater. Feminist propaganda would paint the traditional male roles as more desirable than their own, particularly in the workplace — in the offices, in the factories, in the army and on the police beat — and they began to covet them.

Even the women who had always managed their husbands' pay-cheques (formerly a common practice), and had previously found the greatest satisfaction in their home responsibilities, in the well-being of their families, and in their volunteer concerns for their communities, were soon confused, depressed, and discontented.

Eventually they would be persuaded that men's seemingly inherent characteristics of superior strength, independence, fortitude, and single-minded competitiveness, that led them to patriarchal power — and women's seemingly inherent characteristics of gentleness, kindness, empathy in nurturing and services to family and community, that led them to subjugation and an inferior status — were simply the result of "cultural patterning." Recognizing the androgynous equality of men and women would defeat the former "sexism" in our society, according to feminist doctrine.

Finally, stung by the feminists' nickname for them, "House Slugs," bandied about in the media, many homemakers' discontent flared into personal rage against their subservient role in society, but more directly against those whom they had been told were their oppressors — their husbands.

"Hate" and "vengeance" against the "Male Chauvinist Pigs" suddenly exploded by the fireside. Then began the grand exodus of women from their husbands and homes

— from the loathsome, restraining bonds of duty, discipline, and the unselfish pursuit of family fulfillment — into lives governed only by the goals of self-fulfillment.

Some of these women had their consciousness raised and became successful, rising rapidly beyond their wildest expectations. Others, with great courage and conviction, tried to follow the leaders, but failed and then discovered that they had locked the doors behind them. There were also those women who lingered, hesitant, and then writhed when the census-taker called and they were compelled to admit: "I am just a housewife."

Canadian women returned to pre-marriage occupations in droves, or streamed back into the universities and trade schools for further education and training to fit them for a new lifework. Most of them acknowledged that they were motivated toward the prestige, approbation and power that men were traditionally accorded in the workplace and in the public arenas. Money did not appear to be a primary concern in the exodus of the great numbers of middle-class women, as those women who truly needed their wages were already in the work force. In fact, many surveys have shown that households where both spouses work are often only marginally better off than one-job households — taking into account all added expenses such as the woman's clothes, transportation, day care and restaurant meals.

Still, women's wages and pay equity soon became the foremost issues as the feminists began wresting positions and power away from men. As "hateful" men had "kept women down" for hundreds of years, it was "women's right" now, in the feminists' opinion, to leapfrog deliberately over them, ignoring their years of seniority as well as their constant dedication and experience.

On one of Harry Brown's *Speaking Out* programs on TVOntario, Shirley Carr, then secretary-treasurer of the Canadian Labour Congress, said, "We must sometimes bend the rules." This admission confirmed, conclusively, some of the shocking reports of men with twenty years of seniority and dedication and experience, losing out in promotion opportunities to women with as few as three years' experience, capabilities being considered equal.

I believe that such blatant injustices, as well as the millions of smaller injustices (known, but unacknowledged), that are perpetrated throughout Canadian society today, would lessen if feminists adopted a more reasonable and less vengeful approach. If they studied the historical facts in the evolution of the so-called patriarchy, they might realize that men, generally, were never intentionally subjugating women. Then they might overcome their destructive animosity.

It was only when women's attitudes and aims suddenly changed that they came to see themselves as objects of oppression, of willful subjugation, the victims of gross discrimination and injustices — *not before that time.* Therefore, how can men be indiscriminately condemned and "hated" for being the creators and enforcers of conditions, particularly in the workplace, that preceded the Women's Liberation Movement?

In 1963, the largest proportion of middle-class women on this continent were living in peace in what they believed to be a normal, traditional, worthwhile lifestyle — or if not, then they aspired to that lifestyle.

How many Canadian women twenty years ago wanted to leave their home responsibilities, their motherhood challenges, their comforts, and to some, their great joy in a home setting for the struggles, pressures and seeming glories of sitting in the mahogany chair of the president of a corporation? There were very few. When Betty Friedan claimed they were legion, she was recounting the experience of the discontented present in all occupations. The rest of us had to be taught and ridiculed into imagining that we were "house slugs," and that hedonism, solitary self-fulfillment, and liberation from all home and motherhood responsibilities were worthwhile goals.

There were those women, of course, who were already sitting in the president's chair, or were leaders in law, medicine, and the arts, having risen successfully in the so-called men's world with their own talents and dedicated efforts. Margaret Daly, in an article in *Maclean's Magazine* in 1970, called these women the "enemies of the Women's Liberation Movement... by failing to add their voices to the voice of the Movement, they help to exploit all other women." They were only "token women," she argued. Some such women she named were the following: Dr. Helen Hogg, University of Toronto astronomer; Dr. Marguerite Hill, physician-in-chief of the Women's College Hospital in Toronto; Judy LaMarsh, federal Health Minister and Secretary of State at that time; Toronto police inspector Fern Alexander; and Dodie Robb, the CBC supervisor of daytime programming.[8]

In the United States, feminists continually attacked such women. Susan Sontag wrote in *The Partisan Review:*

The first responsibility of a "liberated" woman is to lead the fullest, freest and most imaginative life she can. The second responsibility is her solidarity with other women. She may live and work and make love with men. But she has no right to represent her situation as simpler, or less suspect, or less full of compromises than it really is. Her good relations with men must not be bought at the price of betraying her sisters.[9]

Laura Legge was one courageous Canadian woman who voiced her objection to this feminist theory. A prominent Toronto lawyer who practices with her husband, Major-General Bruce Legge, and a daughter-in-law, Mary Stokes, she was elected Treasurer of the Law Society of Upper Canada in 1984. She was incensed when a *Chatelaine* columnist wrote: "Mrs. Legge owes some gratitude to the Women's Movement."[10] She pointed out in no uncertain terms that she had been elected by the secret ballots of her peers, fifty-one benchers who had worked closely with her for eight years, and who would never have insulted her with a "token" vote.

The "solidarity of women," of course, has always been a principal platform of feminists in general, and lesbians who have sometimes dominated the Women's Liberation Movement in the United States and Canada in particular — driving wedge after wedge of "hate" and "vengeance" between all women and men. Betty Friedan described homosexuality as "spreading like a murky smog over the American scene," and strongly opposed public support of what she termed the "lavender menace" in 1970 as president of NOW. However, she was to succumb to the influence wielded by the Gay Rights groups in the Women's Liberation Movement, when NOW in 1971 passed the resolutions recognizing the "double oppression of lesbians," and endorsing "child custody rights of mothers who are lesbians."

Militant lesbian feminists are seen to wield similar power in the Canadian Women's Liberation Movement. In Canada, at the three-day conference of the National Action Committee on the Status of Women, in May 1985, the rights of lesbians were again a major issue. Canadian Press, covering the agenda, reported that Canada's largest women's pressure group was demanding "freedom from discrimination for lesbians," and that the government "include sexual orientation as a prohibited ground for discrimination under both federal Human Rights legislation and the Charter of Rights."

Feminists on both sides of the border have campaigned to promote lesbian culture. A Lesbian Herstory Archives Library has been established in New York City, and the International Gay Association sponsored a major conference to study gay culture at the University of Toronto. At the Toronto conference, which dealt with such subjects as homophobia, sodomy and lesbian parenting,

Frances Rooney, editor of *Resources for Feminist Research,* spoke of the urgency of creating a homosexual historical heritage.[11] *The Lesbian Triptych,* written by Quebec author Jovette Marchessault, and translated into English by Yvonne M. Klein, was seen as an important contribution.[12]

In Canada and the United States lesbian feminists are known to be leading other women in demanding artificial insemination by unknown donors, single parenting with social and economic benefits assured, and the acceptance of a "stud culture."

As men and women drift further and further apart, major international studies of the "hate" and "vengeance" factors in the Women's Liberation Movement are being conducted in efforts to understand and explain the consequences. The April 1985 issue of *Psychology Today* carried a detailed report of a cross-continent university study directed by James V.P. Check of York University, Toronto, Neil M. Malamuth of the University of California, Los Angeles, and Barbara Elias and Susan A. Baron of the University of Manitoba, Winnipeg. First of all, the study confirmed that "the problem of hostility between the sexes seems to be a serious one, affecting both men and women."

In the study involving 305 college men and 278 college women, women were asked to reply "true" or "false" to such questions as: "I can easily make a man afraid of me, and sometimes do just for the fun of it," and "Once in a while I cannot control my urge to harm a man." Responses to the "true" or "false" questions in the men's questionnaire seemed to indicate a correlation between loneliness, male hostility, and rape.[13] (In an interview I had with Betty Friedan in the spring of 1985, she suggested that frustrated expectations between the sexes could lead to rape.)

HERizons, a feminist magazine published in Winnipeg, has 10,250 paying subscribers, but relies on federal government business grants to promote its anti-male attacks.

The publication has been labelled "subversive, anti-male, and pro-lesbian" by Manitobans cited in newspaper reports. The Manitoba Association of School Trustees, as well as religious groups, have asked the province to remove it from high school libraries — but to no avail.

One issue of HERizons, considered particularly offensive, ridiculed the Pope's visit to Canada, suggesting that, "an excellent way to respond to the Pope's visit would be to display its absurdity... You might laugh at his costume, his gestures...laughter is a very helpful weapon...." Laughter, scorn, "hate," and "vengeance" have proven a lethal combination.

It becomes very difficult not to believe in the bestiality of the male "animal" with sensational headlines like "One in every ten Canadian men beats his wife, and a like number abuse their children," in newspapers across Canada.

The horrifying figures on child abuse tend not to be questioned, except in the courts that are already dealing with some cases in which fathers have been unjustly accused by mothers seeking sole custody judgements. (Some of those unjustly accused fathers have lost their friends and their businesses, and have had nervous breakdowns, before they were vindicated in the courts.) However, to match statistics of wife abuse by men, should we not have statistics showing how many women are guilty of abusing their husbands, particularly in some of those vicious battles preceding divorce?

Personally, I simply cannot believe that every tenth man I pass on the streets of Toronto, Montreal, St. John's, and Calgary (my own special haunts) is a wife-beater or a child-molester. I know too many good and kind, ordinary Canadian men in all walks of life, including those in my tremendous family connection.

Often I have recognized misleading information, such as that in the published lists of women's groups supposedly belonging to and actively involved in the National Action Committee of the Status of Women Council. In a major article in *The Globe and Mail*, the IODE was listed as one of these, but as a former national officer of IODE, I was able to notify the editors that the old and venerable women's organization, representing thousands of women across Canada, had long since withdrawn from NAC activities. I asked that a clarification also be published, but that request obviously found its way into a wastebasket.

Insisting that all Canadian women are marching in the revolutionary ranks has always been an effective tactic of the Women's Liberation Movement, certainly when it is controlled by powerful feminists in the media.

Only one dissenting voice has succeeded in even being heard, that of an opposing group, calling themselves Real Women of Canada, who claim they speak for a significant number of Canadian women. Still, it is a voice that is consistently drowned out. Real Women are given short shrift when they attempt to lobby government bodies, and are constantly denigrated as "a bunch of pro-life fanatics," in feminist articles, although their interests engage numerous important Canadian problems.

Nevertheless, it is conceivable that there are many more women across the country who would at least stand apart from the "hate" and "vengeance" aspects of the Women's Liberation Movement. Laura Sabia, a prominent Canadian feminist, and the first president of the Ontario Status of Women Council, whom many men have admired as a moderate among radicals, told a Toronto Royal Winter Fair audience on the CBC *Radio Noon Show* hosted by David Shatsky, that presently she was "not as *angry* at men as often as she used to be. . . ." [14]

We must no longer believe that "'man-hating' is an honourable and viable *political* act, that the [so-called] oppressed have a right to class-hatred," as expounded by prominent feminist Patricia Hughes. [15]

3
Evolution and Patriarchy:
A Capsule History

If the modern Women's Liberation Movement can never be recorded as an evolutionary process, but only as a revolution of great design, initiated and executed by some of the most brilliant and dedicated protagonists in history, leading to a matriarchy, there is no evidence that the patriarchy that it will replace throughout the western world, came about in anything but the evolutionary process.

For example, in this century, the tired, mentally and physically scarred men who returned from the bloody battlefields of the two World Wars, seeking solace and approbation from "their" womenfolk, found little resentment among them over their cheerful exodus from the factories and offices. They went back to homes, children, and communities, leaving "their" menfolk to take up again the traditional pattern of the "providers." Only later, in the Sixties, would those same women be persuaded that they should have been resentful at giving up those wartime jobs — which they would then remember as being more prestigious, more lucrative, pleasanter, and much, much easier than homemaking and motherhood, with all their daily physical, mental, and emotional demands.

Historically, men's and women's roles in society were never politicized, or even spelled out. Nor were the lives of men and women ever noticeably disconnected until the eighteenth and nineteenth centuries, with the introduction of the Industrial Age, and the emergence of an enormous urbanized middle class, which was accompanied by the regimentation of society into the opposing classes of capital and labour.

In ancient eras, men and women rose alike in state and family affairs according to their birth or talents. As far back as the second millennium B.C., female pharaohs are known to have ruled Egypt. Hatasu (or Hatshepset) wrested succession to the throne from a half-brother to become Queen of Egypt in 1500 B.C.; she ruled for many decades, and is remembered today for her magnificent obelisks at Thebes, which were financed by treasure-foraging expeditions into Southern Arabia. Of course, Cleopatra was to become the most famous of the queens of Egypt a thousand years later.[1]

There are numerous accounts of powerful queens in Greece, and female tribal leaders throughout Britain and Gaul. During and after the reign of Charlemagne and the Carolingian dynasty of the French kings, queens were reported to be the principal administrators of the realm, one of them particularly noted as being influential as a royal treasurer. From the earliest times, women were engaged in the military campaigns, and during the Middle Ages, when most of the great landowners throughout Europe were away fighting the Crusades, their wives were engaged in defending their families' estates, as well as managing them with great aptitude and skill.

Contrary to some feminist literature, women have always owned large proportions of land in their own names. The Spartan women owned two-fifths of their realm in the fourth century B.C., and in imperial Roman times, women controlled even greater wealth in properties. Later, history would acknowledge that Eleanor of Aquitaine's holdings were much larger than those of King Louis VII of France when she married him, and when that marriage was annulled, the Duchy of Aquitaine was restored to her. It fell under English sovereignty when she became the wife of Henry II in 1152, but she continued as its administrator.

Land and wealth were continually inherited by daughters from their fathers and by wives from their husbands, passed down as often through female lines as male lines, throughout the centuries. Even the Salic Law, one of the earliest Frankish codes, that prohibited female inheritance of property, was largely disregarded, although in some exceptional circumstances it was exercised, as when Edward III of England, through his mother, unsuccessfully challenged the succession of Philip VI to the French throne. This was one of the disputes that triggered the Hundred Years' War.[2]

The other notable application of the Salic Law in history was the separation of Hanover (the German province later annexed to Prussia) and England, when Victoria ascended the British throne in 1837, leaving Ernest Augustus to become King of Hanover. However, beyond Hanover and across the continent, as well as in Britain, women continued to inherit and head enormous estates, while some of the greatest religious communities were established with the wealth of powerful lady abbesses.

Women and men were certainly seen to be equal, and working together, particularly as commerce and trade accelerated across the European continent from the twelfth to the fifteenth century. In England, with the mass exodus from the countryside to the burgeoning towns, women became associated with men, often as partners, in most of the trades and businesses. Sometimes women would be apprentices, assistants, or managers in family workshops, and would carry on such family enterprises in the event of a husband's death. Women were also known to belong to the powerful and exclusive guilds that set standards and regulated trade, and which, in some instances, developed into family strongholds that were to survive until the Industrial Revolution and the divisions of capital and labour.

The great voyages of discovery from western Europe in the fifteenth and sixteenth centuries were followed in the seventeenth and eighteenth centuries by the colonization of all the new lands across the seas, in the settlements where men and women were to support one another in all endeavours.

Pioneer women gained immeasurable respect, usually approaching reverence, as they shared in all the harsh tasks of a primitive society, as well as shouldering the main responsibilities in bearing and rearing the children. However, new expectations and attitudes concerning the male and female roles in family affairs were also exported following the Industrial Revolution in Europe (although America itself did not become truly industrialized until after the Civil War of 1861-65).

These new expectations and attitudes regarding male and female roles, signalled the beginning of a new lifestyle that definitely began to evolve between the middle of the eighteenth and nineteenth centuries in England, as industrialization with all its new technology and economic structures transformed the life of the people.

Wood, water, and wind were replaced by steam, as great a phenomenon in that era as nuclear power in our era. Steamboats and steam engines were introduced, accompanied by the feverish building of canals, railways and roads, while factories sprang up in every corner of the country.

With the invention of the flying shuttle and power looms, there were boom times in the textile towns, with

Yorkshire eventually acknowledged to be the greatest textile centre in the world. The coal mines and new methods of iron production were vital in other manufacturing. Trade experienced giant expansion, particularly in comparison with France, as that country failed to progress while immersed in the problems of the revolution.

Great fortunes were accumulated and these were not in the hands of the aristocrats, who often remained in agriculture on their land holdings. Instead, an enormous middle class developed, as shown in the census figures recorded in those years.[3]

The separation of the sexes that took place at that time among the largest proportion of the population in Britain was a direct result of the better fortunes of that middle class. Furthermore, in many studies, it appears that a patriarchy evolved as a natural condition of the separation.

Men simply began to go off alone to the factories and trade centres, leaving their womenfolk to tend the family homes, raise the children, and care for the communities. These women, as their circumstances were enhanced, adopted new manners and customs, in their new role as full-time chatelaines. At the same time, middle-class men returning to their homes must have imagined themselves as the lords and barons of old — returning from conquests to their own "castles." Their homes and families became increasingly important to them, the very source of all comforts and joys, and it was then they would assume a new mantle, that of a "head" of the home and family, with all the responsibilities of a sole protector and provider.

All members of society came to accept the male role in this sheltered, middle-class setting, with the women often elevated to a pedestal, as the nurturers and guardians of all that the family held dear. Nor did the men always hold the purse strings, (the foremost factor in their domination of women, according to the feminists' claim). It was not at all unusual for the husband-breadwinners to bring their pay-cheques home to their wives, with the wives administering the family funds. This practice was often evident on this continent until women began bringing home their own exclusive pay-cheques during the past two decades. Now, of course, the normal procedure in society accommodates two bank accounts and separated budgets, although a cursory survey of farm women would seem to indicate that a majority of them are still the family accountants, administering family funds from a joint husband-wife bank account.

As the middle class prospered and men and women withdrew into more private and ordered lifestyles, there was a continuing concern for the poor and unattached women working in factories and in other unskilled occupations.

While Charles Dickens was demanding reforms in the employment of children in his famous novels, other renowned reformers, such as Lord Anthony Shaftesbury, were bringing about the abolition of female employment in the mines, as well as limiting their hours in the factories to ten a day. However, in that age, the greatest concern was for women's personal safety, against the moral and spiritual dangers that faced unprotected women in the workplace.[4]   see post · Russia

The new moral codes evolving throughout Queen Victoria's reign, from 1837 to 1901, prescribed rigid standards of behaviour, including chastity before marriage. These were espoused by both men and women of all classes. These codes would be completely denigrated in the modern Women's Liberation Movement as sexually-smothering "Victorianism," and a major factor in the subjugation of women.

Simone de Beauvoir suggested that "the advent of private property" led to the subjugation of women, with the chaste bride and faithful wife also becoming a man's private property. She and her companion, the philosopher Jean-Paul Sartre, were co-editing the Marxist review, *Les Temps Modernes*, in Paris in 1949 when she published her feminist manifesto, *The Second Sex*, with its sensational analysis of the subjugation of women. At that time it was considered pornographic, but it was to endure and serve as a manual for much modern feminist thought on both sides of the Atlantic.[5]

The so-called patriarchy that evolved — with a father-protector-provider, a mother ensuring Victorian principles, a stable home and family atmosphere, and community caring — may have appeared to the majority of the population, particularly in England, as producing an ideal society. Naturally, there were the flaws, the imperfections in the system, noticeably in the men who became tyrants — tyrants in family life, tyrants in government, tyrants in the workplace. When one of these men was identified, even if he were one of 100,000, he would prove fair game for the feminists, illustrating the evils in a patriarchal society. Personal experiences undoubtedly led to public outcries.

Mary Wollstonecraft, who is credited with writing the first great feminist protest against men's dominance over women, in *The Vindication of Women*, published in 1792, claimed she had a tyrannical father, whose misfortunes in business she treated with the utmost contempt. She had also "rescued" her sister Eliza from a tyrannical husband — although this was questioned later by Eliza when she expressed bitter resentment at her sister's interference and the attempted destruction of her marriage.

There were other men Mary Wollstonecraft hated, including her brother, Ned, of whom she was violently jealous. He was her mother's favourite, and was to inherit money and become a successful lawyer, all because he was a "privileged male," in her eyes. Her disastrous affair with Gilbert Imlay, the American with whom she lived in Paris during the French Revolution, who deserted her following the birth of their daughter, Fanny, enraged and embittered her. She believed in freedom, the "liberation" of women from all men. Yet, in her last few months of life she was seemingly happily married to William Godwin, her publisher. She died in 1797, giving birth to another Mary, who was also to become a famous author, and most loving wife of the English poet, Percy Bysshe Shelley. Many of the elder Mary's readers would remember, ironically, that she had finally extolled marriage as "the foundation of almost every social virtue," potentially a "microcosm of social harmony."[6]

ON THIS CONTINENT

There were certainly no deliberate efforts toward the "liberation" of women from men, and "freedom" from their domination in the suffrage movements that developed as early as the mid-1880s in the United States. It was the great social issues of the times that initially inspired women to look beyond their families and homes to become involved in social reforms, which they realized would have to be accomplished through government legislation — and therefore their vote. Furthermore, it is important to note that there were always men supporting women in their suffrage campaigns in Canada and the United States, as there were in England, even during the bloody battles of the Pankhursts. There are numerous accounts of meetings in which the numbers of suffragists equalled the numbers of suffragettes.

In the United States, it was the abomination of slavery that women rose to attack, led by two beautiful southern women. Sarah and Angelina Grimké, daughters of a South Carolina slave-holding family, were to become famous early in the nineteenth century, with their combined efforts to draw attention to a custom they abhorred. Moving to Philadelphia, they became associated with organized abolitionist groups, under such influential leaders as John Greenleaf Whittier and Theodore Weld (whom Angelina eventually married). Under the auspices of the American Anti-Slavery Society, they began speaking throughout New York and New England, bringing a first-hand description of slavery to their listeners.[7]

When multitudes of women espoused the cause, they came to believe that women could hasten reform by direct participation in government. "Women's right" to vote, to have a distinctive voice in making and changing the laws of the land, became imperative, and the two causes were linked, again supported by prominent male legislators. When one of these men arranged to have Angelina Grimké appear before a government committee of the Massachusetts State House, she would be the first woman in America to speak before a legislature.

There were always men supporting women as they moved toward female suffrage, and there was never violence in this movement in the United States and Canada, such as the pitched battles and jail terms suffered by the suffragettes in England. For instance, at the historic Seneca Falls Convention in 1848, when Elizabeth Cady Stanton delivered her maiden speech in a tiny Wesleyan chapel, in which she demanded "women's sacred right to the elective franchise," the 300 women present were joined by forty uninvited men, and thirty-two of them signed the renowned Declaration of Principles. Former President of the United States, John Quincy Adams, known in his later years as "Old Man Eloquent," had also provided a powerful voice on women's behalf, with his wife, Abigail, becoming a suffragette.[8]

Temperance, of course, was another great social issue, which concerned women of both sides of the border, who were soon persuaded that they must be allowed a voice in public affairs to express their concern. As the manufacture and sale of liquor were controlled by government, the liquor laws had to be changed. As the "law grows out of the will of majorities, and majorities of women are against the liquor traffic," the women's franchise became the crucial issue.[9]

The Women's Christian Temperance Union was founded in 1874 in Cleveland, Ohio, and was soon attracting membership across the country, under the dynamic leadership of Frances Willard, a former president of the Evanston (Illinois) College for Ladies, and later, when that was absorbed into Northwestern University, Dean of the Women's College. In 1878, Miss Willard combined the two issues, temperance and the women's franchise, in a petition she presented to the Illinois State Legislature with 180,000 names — and approximately half of those signatures were those of men.[10]

"Home Protection" drives against all the dangers in the liquor trade were organized throughout the country, with chapters of the W.C.T.U. springing up in the largest and smallest centres. Abolition had been achieved, the Civil War was over, and American women would now turn with all their energies against this other great evil, with increasing demands for the female franchise to effect reform.

The National Woman Suffrage Association had been launched in 1869 by Mrs. Stanton and Susan B. Anthony (the latter, a daughter of the famous Quaker abolitionist, Daniel Anthony, had also fought in the anti-slavery cause) to agitate for an amendment to the federal Constitution. The same year, Lucy Stone, founder of the respected *Woman Suffrage Magazine,* led another group, the American Association, to lobby state legislatures. It would be the women of the west who were to make the greatest progress, with state after state granting suffrage to women within their borders, Wyoming leading in 1869.[11]

In 1911, a Men's League for Woman Suffrage was organized, aiding in the long and cumbersome process of amendments to state and federal legislation. With the participation of women in the war efforts of World War I, all political parties were committed to their enfranchisement, and the federal amendment to the American Constitution giving women the vote was finally laboured through Congress in 1920.

It must be remembered that suffrage seemed of little importance to women prior to the mid-nineteenth century, as it had been primarily associated with property, and was only exercised by a small class of men and women who owned property. (French-Canadian women with considerable holdings were voting in Quebec well into the nineteenth century.)

In Canada it was also the social issues of the times that motivated women toward involvement in public affairs, and seeking an effective voice in legislation. Furthermore, as in the United States, it was in the west where pioneer women first achieved full provincial suffrage — in Manitoba in 1916, closely followed by legislation in Alberta, Saskatchewan and British Columbia in that same year.

The Canadian Woman Suffrage Movement was actually born in a small Toronto Literary Club, founded in 1876 by Dr. Emily Howard Stowe, Canada's first woman physician. But it was two western journalists and social reformers, Nellie McClung and Emily Murphy, who brought the Canadian crusade to fruition, with the Dominion franchise granted in 1918.

Both women emigrated from Ontario, Nellie McClung to Manitoba with her family in 1880, and Emily Murphy to Alberta in 1907. They joined forces and became nationally known as the principal petitioners in the historic "Persons Case" of 1929, in which the High Court in London finally ruled that women were persons in the Constitution, despite statutory wording that was held to deny women "personhood." Their success in this case would signal a "symbolic end to the Equal Rights struggle in English Canada." But Emily Murphy's earlier efforts were recognized in 1916, when she was appointed police magistrate in Edmonton, the first such appointment made in the British Empire.[12]

Nellie McClung had joined the W.C.T.U. in 1897, and never ceased in her efforts to redeem society from the devastating effects of alcoholism. She also belonged to the Methodist Epworth League, as well as working with J.S.Woodsworth in Winnipeg's All People's Mission, attacking all the problems of a burgeoning city, with its great influx of non-Anglo-Saxon immigrants and its sweat shops. Hardship in the surrounding rural areas was also her major continuing concern. Her war efforts with the Red Cross and Patriotic Fund were rewarded by her appointment by Prime Minister Sir Robert Borden, to the Canadian War Conference in 1918. In 1921, she ran successfully for the Alberta legislature where she championed temperance, public health, rural improvements and women's rights in all governing bodies.

In all Nellie McClung's writings, both in her books and in magazine articles, she suggested that women's deeper sensibilities and "moral superiority" gave them greater awareness of human suffering and needs, and therefore that "Women must be made to feel their responsibilities...must at last emerge from the home and use their special talents to serve and save the race." She urged that their "instinctive mother love, be organized in some way, and made effective. There was enough of it in the world to do away with all the evils which war upon childhood, undernourishment, slum conditions, child labour, drunkenness. Women could abolish all these if they wanted to," she preached.[13]

"The mothering ideal was central to McClung's feminism....She regarded motherhood as the highest achievement of her sex." Furthermore, she argued that "Women needed a harmonious home life in order to take on outside activities," according to Veronica Strong-Boag's biographical introduction to a 1972 edition of Nellie McClung's *In Times Like These*. In addition to her "harmonious home life" and constant encouragement from her husband, Nellie McClung was always confident of the support of western men, individually and in powerful city and farm groups.

There is no evidence that any of the early feminists seeking suffrage, on this continent at least, saw any evil in the so-called "patriarchal" system — in which men, generally, were required to protect, and pull the heaviest loads, with homes and children designated as women's primary responsibility. The words "patriarchy" and "liberation" (from men), and that slogan "Down with Men," were never heard in those early campaigns for "women's rights." Nor would any of those early feminists ever have sanctioned the resulting dissolution of traditional lifestyles and the destruction of families that have followed the modern feminist revolution.

As women espoused community and national causes in the suffrage movements, they did not leave their homes but looked beyond them, to see the social ills, to effect reforms, to change the laws — these actions required their enfranchisement. This would be an extension of women's work on school and welfare boards, and their volunteer services in women's organizations such as the revered IODE and Women's Institutes, organizations that had attracted all classes of women, and spread into every hamlet from coast to coast, from their inception in 1900. Getting the government to accept women in a new law-making role — casting their vote — would be a tedious process. Many women considered women's suffrage the ultimate triumph, achieving equality in a vote for the vote. Actually, there were 9.4 million more women than men entitled to vote in the United States in 1982, according to an American Census Bureau report.

It seems basically unjust that the role of men in all women's endeavours toward suffrage in Europe and on this continent has been conveniently buried by revolutionary feminists in the past two decades, in their campaign to vilify men generally in a so-called insufferable patriarchy. Yet it was a man who was the very originator of the women's suffrage movement, in the opinion of many.

The Pankhurst women have become the most famous in feminist history, as the leaders of the British movement, and as having the greatest influence in the American and Canadian movements. This was largely through their lectures and the publicity of their exploits, the pitched battles with police, the jail terms and hunger strikes. But it was Emmeline's husband, Christabel's and Sylvia's father, Richard Pankhurst, who established the principles, and created the first programs of the movement.

A brilliant radical lawyer, and Member of Parliament from Manchester, Richard Pankhurst began by founding the Women's Franchise League. His Married Women's Property Bill became law in 1882. In 1884, he was instrumental in having the Local Government Act passed, giving women the local franchise. He was deeply involved in other efforts for women's rights at the time of his death in 1898, but his wife and daughters continued to carry on the work.[14]

We must also remember that it was women who often posed the greatest opposition to woman suffrage, on both continents. In England, Queen Victoria proved an implacable enemy to the cause, with her chief ministers, Gladstone and Disraeli, dutifully blocking legislation. And on this continent, there were always the women who would stand, unyielding in their belief that women's role and responsibilities were primarily in motherhood and family affairs. They would finally come to understand that the franchise could simply mean an extension of women's family caring outward to the community.

Certainly, the majority of women in the 1920s must have been convinced that they had achieved an ultimate goal, throughout the United States and Canada (Quebec, alone, with its French-Canadian and devout Catholic traditions, would withhold the provincial women's franchise until 1940). More women with particular ambitions and talents chose careers in all areas of society, and when their attributes matched or surpassed the dogged determination and dedication of some men, they also gained fame or fortune or both, long before the modern Women's Liberation Movement demanded that biological considerations be ignored, and that all women cultivate androgynous ambitions and challenging spirits.

The *Encyclopaedia Britannica*, in the 1962 edition, recorded that women no longer faced any "substantial limitations" in regard to public office or property rights:

> Women hold the most exalted public offices. They have been governors of several states, members of the United States Senate and House of Representatives, members of the president's cabinet and judges in both the federal courts and the courts of many of the states. Indeed, there is no legal obstacle to the election of a woman as president or vice-president of the United States. [15]

This was a recording of facts, and yet, one year later, in 1963, women across the continent were being persuaded in Betty Friedan's book, *The Feminine Mystique*, and later in all the onslaughts of the feminist revolution, of their disadvantages, of their lack of equality, of the domination of men, and of their need to be "liberated" from all the constraints of an evil and unacceptable patriarchy.

4
Revolution and Matriarchy

While there is ample evidence that patriarchy came about in a purely evolutionary process, in no way can the Women's Liberation Movement, leading to matriarchy, be judged as evolutionary either in Canada or in the United States. Clearly it can be seen as an inspired social revolution, with all the dynamics of a crusade, founded on a philosophy demanding the recognition of absolute sex equality in all areas of society. It is dedicated to the eradication of all the sexist forms of injustice and oppression, as perceived by the feminists, of a former patriarchy.

"I did not set out consciously to start a revolution when I wrote *The Feminine Mystique,*" Betty Friedan admitted in her introduction to her second book, *It Changed My Life,* published in 1975. However, the Women's Liberation Movement, which she launched, developed into "possibly the most far-reaching revolution of all time," in her own words:

It affects our daily personal lives immediately,

women, men, children; pervades all our institutions, office and home; confronts the economy,
politics of right and left, theology, sexuality itself,
in unpredictable ways...We otherwise ordinary
American women, finding the power to change our
own lives, changed the face of history.[1]

That this powerful writer could convince the majority
of the women of her time that their traditional values
and lifestyles were worthless, must finally be acknowledged as the historical phenomenon of all time. There
were many women, of course, who would read *The
Feminine Mystique* in 1963 in disbelief, denying its
principal concepts. These concepts seemed to have been
based on the experiences of wretchedly unhappy, frustrated, and deprived housewives, while the purposeful
wives and mothers who may have considered homemaking
a most satisfying and rewarding occupation were never
considered in the book or in any of the subsequent literature of the Women's Liberation Movement. Denigrating
a woman's traditional role in marriage, motherhood, and
homemaking, as well as in her volunteer community
efforts, would always be the principal platform in the
revolution.

The Feminist Mystique compared the housewife with a
prisoner in a Nazi concentration camp:

It is urgent to understand how the very condition
of being a housewife can create a sense of emptiness,
non-existence, nothingness, in women. There are
aspects of the housewife role that make it almost
impossible for a woman of adult intelligence to
retain a sense of human identity, the firm core of
self or "I" without which a human being, man or
woman, is not truly alive. For women of ability, in
America today, I am convinced there is something
about the housewife state itself that is dangerous...

the women who "adjust" as housewives, who grow up wanting to be "just a housewife," are in as much danger as the millions who walked to their own death in the concentration camps....

Strangely enough, the conditions which destroyed the human identity of so many prisoners were not the torture and the brutality, but conditions similar to those which destroy the identity of the American housewife.... The prisoners were forced to adopt childlike behaviour... forced to give up their individuality and merge themselves into an amorphous mass... forced to spend their days in work which produced great fatigue — not because it was physically killing, but because it was monotonous, endless, required no mental concentration, gave no hope of advancement or recognition, was sometimes senseless and was controlled by the needs of others....[2]

The women who would read and believe this description of their lives and goals would also find the key to open the doors to new lives and goals, in Betty Friedan's words that disparaged control by "the needs of others." Henceforth, "the needs of others" must be subordinated to their own needs, their own desires, their own aims, their own satisfaction.

The Women's Liberation Movement was born, and women's lives were certainly transformed — wives and mothers were liberated from the needs of husbands, children, homes, and communities. If they hesitated, or their wills weakened, these women were able to use the force and energy of new-found anger to propel them into their new lives, anger directed particularly against their husbands, their first targets. As their eyes were opened to recognize a patriarchy, these women saw their husbands as the oppressors and themselves as the oppressed, the most disadvantaged members of society. Later, women generally would be sexually "liberated," persuaded by such writers as Germaine Greer.

While Betty Friedan claimed that she had simply struck a chord in women's lives — their response eventually was to turn their backs on lifestyles they had formerly held dear — there were still homemakers across the land who could dismiss all the ensuing feminist teachings, never doubting the purpose of their own lives or the worth of their commitments. To them, marriage and motherhood was the most complex and difficult (and most rewarding) of all occupations. They judged the feminists as malcontents, unhappily inadequate to all the challenges, who would attempt to persuade all other women to return to their pre-marriage state of ordered, comparatively easy, one-dimensional lives, in stores, in offices, in boardrooms, in factories, with the hated housework no longer a woman's sole responsibility, and the care of their children, as in Marxist theory, to be finally funded by government. (Betty Friedan has written extensively of her own frustrations, unhappiness, and guilt as she struggled to find herself and her priorities in early married life.)

However, there were no dissenting voices. There may have been a silent majority disbelieving the impetus of the onslaught, but there was no great writer, in those years from 1963 to 1970, with rhetoric comparable to Betty Friedan's in *The Feminine Mystique*, who would tell a different story of the lives and times of other women.

Speculation is wasteful, yet compelling. One must always wonder, if other views had found equal airing, would the Women's Liberation Movement have continued in the hands of the moderates, moderates who might have striven as diligently and as successfully, but with greater justice, towards the reasonable goals of equal opportunities in education and the workplace, particularly for those women who were espousing the new attitudes? Instead, of course, it would fall into the hands of the militants and the fanatics, who would orchestrate, pell-mell, the mass disruptions and desolation of a revolution, allowing no choices.

While the matriarchy moves inexorably into position in Canada, with every new program encouraged and funded, there are certainly other views opposing immoderacy now being heard throughout the United States. At the same time, those forgotten, but dedicated homemakers, who have been resisting the feminist tides, are gaining courage — raising their heads again — to demand recognition and respect for their traditional work and lifestyles, centred in the home.

For example, Janet Scott Barlow was one of the first American writers to express the opinions of such women, in a major article in the prestigious magazine, *Commonweal.* She wrote:

> My first child and my first real awareness of the Women's Movement arrived together in 1970. Since then I have followed my nature, my needs, and my personal commitment, and have remained a fulltime mother....."Fulltime" meaning all the work, all the care, all the time (with help from my husband after his day at his fulltime job). Fulltime in spite of the fact that my household could have used a second income. Fulltime because I thought I could be a "complete" person and raise my children at the same time....
>
> During the early, highly vocal years of the Women's Movement, mothers who chose to stay home with their children were used as negative symbols.... Fulltime motherhood was characterized as confining, relentless, nerve-stripping and mind-deadening — all of which was partly true, some of the time. Left untouched was the fact that amidst the confinement and relentlessness and stripped nerves and

deadened minds were large nuggets of genuine reward and satisfaction found nowhere else in life. Totally ignored was the fact a woman who can help to instill in her growing children compassion and courage and honor and humor, while also managing housework and homework and carpools and illness, and do it all day, every day, year after year, is a woman who *knows* something. Things being what they are, she is also a woman who needs to be *told* that she knows something.

Mothers needed to hear aloud a truth that existed in their own minds and hearts, but seemed to exist few other places: that the commonplace work of raising children had value — not dollar value, but social value, personal value, moral value...that all human endeavor has a cost....

This American writer was convinced that the Women's Liberation Movement had conclusively defamed motherhood in its determination to drive all women from their homes. "Women were told that they were suppressing their *Selves* and living through their children. They knew it was a lie..." she wrote.

The condition of motherhood is one of life's ultimate inescapable facts. The essence of being a mother is a woman's awareness that for as long as she lives, she will be bound to her children by her own intimate love and concern and hope. Some of the by-products of this awareness are human insight, philosophical and psychological resilence, and the instinct to know what's important and what isn't.[3]

There were thousands of other homemakers "out there" who may have recognized these assumptions, and whose experiences and views could have been recorded to balance those recorded in *The Feminine Mystique* and other feminist writings. I was one of them, a successful journalist who had written for daily newspapers and trade journals, but had left an editor's position on a national magazine for homemaking. I was then too engrossed with all the complexities, challenges and joys of marriage and motherhood to pay proper attention to the feminist revolution that was toppling age-old traditions and former "feminine" lifestyles. Not that I ever ignored the outside world, as I was always involved in volunteer work with IODE (the national women's organization that was building community halls and health stations throughout Canada's most northern lands; aiding Indian and ethnic groups in all Canadian cities; founding historical societies in preserving Canadian culture; and presently building community and day care centres in Labrador).

Actually, I chose my lifestyle twice. When my youngest child was five and happily off to school, CBC's Andrew Simon offered me a job as a radio interviewer, and with great enthusiasm I began CBC's diction lessons with the famous actress, Beth Lockerbie. However, after only a few completed programs, suddenly one of my children came down with a serious illness. Again I faced my own priorities, and quit interviewing.

At the same time I have numerous women friends and relatives who are teachers, nurses, doctors, and lawyers — and also marvellous mothers, perfectly capable of managing two careers. Their natures comprise dispositions, emotions, and attitudes which I am convinced provide them with special skills. In many cases, they chose their own lifestyles long before the feminist revolution. There have always been Margaret Thatchers and Golda Meirs, although it must be pointed out that many such women *did not seek their potential* in the workplace until their children had reached certain ages. (In a true

Ottawa story, Jean Piggott was able to persuade Cabinet Minister Pat Carney to run for a federal seat only after she had promised hot lunches for a teen-age son!)

It is not a truly free society if women are not allowed to make their own choices — unintimidated by feminist theories that define what "work" is important. American author Barbara Grizzuti Harrison asked, in a *Harper's Magazine* article: "What is the real work of the world? If the real work of the world is that which extends into the future, that which is not ephemeral, and that which sustains life, we are talking about poetry and bread and babies, not (one supposes) about finance and guns."[4]

The Women's Liberation Movement never, apparently, took into consideration the unique individuality of women. With disbelief, I have listened to militant feminists attempt to drive all women, like a herd of cattle, into the same corral, allowing no choices.

It is true that some women with exceptional talents required prodding to develop them, while others needed their "consciousness raised" (a catch phrase of the revolution) to recognize and develop self-interest, and ambitions. No one has ever faulted efforts to establish equal opportunities in education, opportunities now heavily weighted in favour of women.

Canadian women are still being driven, by contempt and derision, into believing that the most important work is outside the home, particularly in formerly male-dominated occupations, including company management, factory management, union management, truck and taxi driving and army combat. While American women psychologists and writers are beginning to question this belief, no prominent Canadian woman psychologist or writer has yet pointed out that the most difficult, demanding, confusing, messy, menial, ecstatically satisfying, joy-producing, and challenging work in the world can be found by some women in the home, in marriage and motherhood.

Feminist militants can be the most outrageous liars when they continually argue that homemaking is a luxury, only for the well-to-do. Personally, I am intimate with the happy, satisfying, rewarding lifestyles of extremely poor housewives, relatives and friends, even young home-makers living near the poverty line. Some of them with highly marketable skills claim they are simply willing to forgo better homes, better clothes, and restaurant meals, at least while their children are small.

Misconstruing facts has been a lethal weapon in the revolution, as often practised by popular feminist colum-nists. It was the "homemaking is only for the rich" argument that Lois Sweet used when some mothers actually wrote to *The Toronto Star* with views different from hers. She had asked for "readers' comments about the frustration working parents face when confronting nine teachers' professional development days each year...."

One mother wrote:

My main point of concern is that you, like many other working mothers, "want to have your cake and eat it too." On the one hand, you want the extra income, while at the same time you *expect* someone else to look after your children on a five-day-a-week basis and are angry if you are inconvenienced to any extent — nothing must interfere with your income, not even the care of your children...! You are just plain greedy.

Lois Sweet replied:

Let's face it: There's always an ideal — and then there's reality. In an ideal world, all parents would have the *luxury* [my italics] of staying home with their children, people would work only by choice (and at totally satisfying, socially productive jobs). . . . In reality, however, most people work to feed and clothe their children, not to buy yachts. . . .[5]

It is true that there are swelling numbers of single mothers who must support their children. Job training, jobs that raise their standard of living, and state-provided day care must be the only solution in their particular situations. "But to suggest that we housewife-mothers who *chose* homemaking as a lifestyle (and these are dwindling numbers in the matriarchy), belong to a no-purpose 'yachts class,' is insulting," one young, poor but happy housewife-mother remarked. She also admitted cheerfully that she had long since stopped reading feminist articles, including those featured in *Chatelaine* every month. "Why do they still call it *Chatelaine?*" she wondered.

Closing their eyes on the Women's Liberation Movement has been the only defence of many women with opposing views, and yet this may be explained in the words of the philosopher, C.G. Jung: "The insignificance of the individual is rubbed into him so thoroughly that he loses all hope of making himself heard." Jung also said: "Resistance to the organized mass can be effected only by the man who is as well-organized in his individuality as the mass itself."[6] After all, institutions as well as persons have fallen before the onslaughts of the feminist "masses."

Tracking the course of the feminist revolution in Canada will undoubtedly be done in future historical studies of great depth, but all of them must take into account the backgrounds, convictions, motives, and directions of the leading protagonists. Only in such studies may we come to understand fully the most powerful forces that are reshaping conclusively every area of Canadian life. There is already locked-in legislation in place or promised in every province across the country, with every feminist program reinforced, promoted, and funded at the federal level.

Feminism in Canada, a book of essays and lectures published by Black Rose Books Ltd. of Montreal, clearly spells out the feminist theories and revolutionary goals of English- and French-speaking university professors with academic authority. In an introduction, editor Angela R. Miles, who teaches sociology at St. Francis Xavier University in Antigonish, Nova Scotia, and is active in women's studies,[7] proclaimed:

> The authors of the articles here are, by label, social-ist, Marxist, lesbian, radical and anarchist femi-nists.... The authors all presume that feminist revolution/evolution will involve a total integrative restructuring of society and human relations....
>
> Their emphasis on reproduction-related and female-associated values as the key to feminist social change takes their critiques of established social science, psychology, economics, history, anthropol-ogy, philosophy, social work, politics and political theory, beyond proscription to prescription. In the process of criticizing established disciplines and politics, most of these articles lay out guidelines for the development of feminist scholarship and politics.[8]

Strategies in the revolutionary struggle are also "pre-scribed" by such women of authority in universities from coast to coast. Co-editor Geraldine Finn, who focussed her Master's and Doctoral studies on Marxism, pheno-menology and structuralism, has taught philosophy at the CEGEP de l'Outaouais Heritage Campus in Hull, Quebec, since 1975.[9] In *Feminism in Canada*, she states that "All the contributors agree... that feminism is revolutionary and that the feminist revolution will be a total one, leaving no aspect of social life unchanged...."

In describing "the strategic approach to the destruc-tion of patriarchal social structures espoused by the writers of these articles," Geraldine Finn quoted Grace MacInnis. "There are... two ways of getting rid of a structure.... One is to put a bomb under it... and the other is to dig around and undermine it till it topples," the latter being considered the most viable. This quotation is attributed to a feature by Dorothy Livesay, "The Woman Writer and The Idea of Progress," published in November 1982, in the *Canadian Forum*, a monthly magazine funded by the Canada Council.

Women are advised to fight

> *on all fronts at once*... There is no linchpin to patriarchal power; no Winter Palace which can be assaulted collectively and appropriated once and for all — though all the contributors [in *Feminism in Canada*] are united in their recognition of the control of reproduction as one of its fundamental constituents. The mechanisms of male dominance are multiform and interconnected (they have had a long time to grow and consolidate) — the family, the economy, the church, and the educational system, for example. These pivotal points of control have to be *undermined*, not merely assaulted, but dismantled bit-by-bit from the ground up.[10]

Mary O'Brien, a Scottish immigrant, formerly active in the British Labour Party, with a Ph.D. in political theory, began teaching feminist studies at the Ontario Institute for Studies in Education in 1977. In her lectures and writings "she seeks to integrate feminist concern with the social relations of reproduction and Marxist analysis of class relations." In her chapter on "Feminism and Revolution," she expounds: "I believe that the critique of male supremacy which can uncover the revolutionary structure of women's history and create a living feminist praxis must be conducted from within Marxism."[11] She also sees "several identifiable strains within feminism which have anarchical connotations; the insistence that the personal is political is one of these, and the rejection of hierarchical modes of organization is another." She repeats Carol Ehrlich's arguments that the "basic tasks for feminism are well defined: 'Destroy Capitalism, End Patriarchy, Smash Heterosexism.'"[12]

Mary O'Brien's recurring theme, however, like that of Simone de Beauvoir, the famous French feminist, concerns reproduction. In 1949, Simone de Beauvoir, then co-editor of the Marxist review, *Les Temps Modernes*, published *The Second Sex*, in which she saw reproduction as the principal cause of women's subjugation by men. Mary O'Brien is repetitive in the anthology, but explains her thesis at greater length in her book, *The Politics of Reproduction*. She states that

> it is not within sexual relations but within *the total process of human reproduction* that the ideology of male supremacy finds its roots and its rationales.... It is from an adequate understanding of the process of reproduction, nature's traditional and bitter trap for the suppression of women, that women can begin to understand their possibilities and their freedoms.[13]

Men in the new society are considered by Patricia Hughes who has a Ph.D. in political theory from the University of Toronto and an LL.B. from Osgoode Law School. A member of the Feminist Party of Canada and the Toronto Area Caucus of Women and the Law, she is involved with the Canadian Abortion Rights Action League, and was active in a New Democratic Party federal candidacy in the 1979 election.[14] Her thoughts and reasoning seem to be in line with the very basic doctrines of the Women's Liberation Movement:

> Goodness knows feminists have plenty of concerns to occupy our time and our minds without worrying

about the fate of men in the feminist movement. Yet it is an issue that is not easily dismissed, for both moral and strategic reasons....

Feminism holds that women's oppression is founded in patriarchy: male-dominated, male-defined assumptions and institutions. It is important to note that in speaking of male values or male institutions, we are speaking of an ideology; it is true that the ideology and the individuals coincide and that all men benefit in some way from their status as males in a patriarchy, but the focus of our feminist ideology should be masculinist ideology or malism. Thus we seek our release and self-affirmation through the act of overthrowing or transcending male political, economic, and legal institutions, male concepts, male values, and male culture....

But feminism is far from being merely destructive of malism, for self-affirmation can truly arise only out of creation, not out of destruction. Feminism entails a vision which contemplates a metamorphosis of society along feminist principles.... This means that while feminist practice does not *require* men, it must recognize their existence and determine their place in the theory and in the practice because they, too, will be a part of feminist society. [15]

There are many authoritative books such as *Feminism in Canada* to be read in the Women's Studies courses, courses that continue to flourish and multiply in all the universities in Canada. The professors and lecturers involved may come to be recognized as the most powerful influence in the Women's Liberation Movement — the very builders of the new society, the matriarchy.

In the United States, Dr. George Gelded, author of a best-selling book, *Sexual Terrorism*, claims that every year "25,000 inocent co-eds are transformed into dedicated ruthless libbers," in the Women's Studies courses in American universities. "These courses constitute the most brutal brainwashing since Joseph Stalin introduced compulsory nursery school in the Soviet Union,"[16] in his opinion. And yet, feminist professors and lecturers in the general disciplines may wield an even greater influence.

The subtle persuasion to follow blindly the "brainy" leadership of such feminists is also apparent in innumerable media articles. Doris Anderson, in a prominent piece in *The Toronto Star,* seems to be promoting the lifestyle of women who are "choosing to go it alone as mothers" — with unknown fathers and artificial insemination. The women she features in that article are of superior intellect and education:

> Catherine L. is one of a growing number of women in their 30s — more than three times as many as in 1974 — who have opted to have and raise a child on their own.... [She is] a well-established accountant, five months pregnant through artificial insemination, unmarried, and planning to raise her baby by herself... confident she can manage both physically and financially...."A lot of women do end up raising sons by themselves and do a good job, so why can't I?" she asks with quiet confidence.
>
> Nancy S., 34 years old, a Ph.D and a university lecturer, has had three miscarriages and is trying once again.... She has never met the prospective father of her child. The arrangements were made through friends....
>
> Both women know other women, like themselves, who are having children alone. A pediatrician took four months off and now works part time; a psychiatrist decided to have a child with a friend who lives in Montreal.[17]

Women readers with less education and meaner qualifications could still be persuaded that this is a desirable route for them as well. Furthermore, the "rights" of such offspring to know their fathers and benefit from association with a male parent are not included in the Charter of Rights in our Canadian Constitution, nor is it likely they will be sought in the courts in our new society. Women's "rights" would always take precedence, including the right to choose this calculated form of reproduction.

While articles as suggestive as Doris Anderson's occasionally may have far-reaching effects in the lives of the readers, it is in the courses, classes, and seminars, particularly in Women's Studies, in all the universities, that young women, daily, are being taught the beliefs, principles, and strategies of the Women's Liberation Movement. Feminist women professors must often become their role models, replacing former role models, such as mothers.

Eager young women's-libbers might accept Patricia Hughes' theory, that "feminist practice does not *require* men." However, they must remember that this prominent lawyer and political activist also reasons and writes that "oppressed peoples...must decide whether to redefine separation so that it benefits themselves, or to seek to bring members of the tyrannical group into some kind of harmonious and integrated relationship."[18]

There are probably few feminists on either side of the border who are actually endorsing the scientific studies now underway in the United States to determine how to "create life without males." Until recently, scientists claimed that only the most primitive life forms, such as certain bacteria, could live a true unisex life — that anything "complex enough to have a skeleton, needed both genders" for reproduction. Their thinking was to be radically altered with the discovery of about twenty species of lizards in the southwestern United States, in northern Mexico and in Russia's Caucasus mountains, all of them female and thriving without males.

Professor Clement Markert, director of the Center for

Reproductive Biology at Yale University, has described the creatures as laying eggs "which hatch into females, which grow up and lay eggs, which hatch into females...." Scientists have documented what these lizards do that is different from other species in producing offspring, but have been unable to analyze the process. Nevertheless, Professor Markert and other researchers are convinced that eventually they will be able to duplicate the process in their laboratories, pointing toward a whole new concept of reproduction. [19]

Of course, if these studies prove fruitful, they must certainly hold promise of a great future for lesbians, who are still increasing in numbers and influence in the American and Canadian Women's Liberation Movements.

At the 1985 conference of the National Organization of Women (NOW) in New Orleans, 25 per cent of the delegates were lesbians, a figure that the newly elected president, Eleanor Smeal concedes (while emphasizing that she herself is a wife and a mother). [20] Many years ago, the lesbian members of NOW were successful in having homosexuality removed from the list of neuroses by both the American Psychological and Psychiatric Associations, opening the floodgates for all gays.

In Canada, voting delegates to the annual meeting of the National Action Committee of the Status of Women (NAC) agreed to lobby the government to include sexual orientation as a prohibited ground for discrimination both under federal human rights legislation and in the Charter of Rights. (*The Globe and Mail*, May 13, 1985).

Canadian unions are also championing lesbian causes, as in the case of Karen Andrews, a 25-year-old Toronto library worker, who lives with her lover and two children, and is determined that the arrangement be considered a family, eligible for employee benefits, such as medical and dental coverage, including orthodontics, and pensions. She is backed by her union, the Canadian Union of Public Employees, and CUPE lawyers were soon able to achieve at least partial coverage, paid for by the library board, while they continue to pursue complete family benefits in this homosexual situation.[21] (The cost of accommodating lesbians in this and other areas, could be astronomical in regulatory management, as their relationships often may be transient.)

I have heard some feminists declare that specific lesbian causes should all be fought for outside the Women's Liberation Movement. They deplore the influence of lesbians who have commandeered the spotlight and feminist energies regularly for their own advancement.

"Sisterhood" has become the latest battle-cry in the feminist revolution, following "consciousness-raising" and "self-affirmation." It seems ironic that women, after all their revolutionary struggles to break down the barriers of all-male bastions, in occupations, organizations, and national and community clubs, are now clustering from coast to coast in large and small, all-female, no-males-allowed, groups.

For example, traditionally in Ontario, there have always been male and female elementary school teachers' associations, such as the Federation of Women Teachers' Associations of Ontario, founded in 1918. However, in 1972, succumbing to the pressures of the Women's Liberation Movement, the men teachers opened the doors of their previously all-male Ontario Public School Teachers' Federation to the women, and in 1985, Mary Hill, an Ottawa-area vice-principal, became president of that organization, which now comprises 14,000 male and 800 female teachers. At the same time, the women have steadfastly refused to accept men into their membership, as well as resisting all overtures of the male teachers who have been trying during the past twenty years to persuade them to amalgamate.[22]

Gloria Steinem, the foremost American feminist, who in 1972 co-founded the popular feminist magazine Ms., described as the bible of the Women's Liberation Move-

or mirror image

ment in the United States, now constantly emphasizes the importance of "sisterhood" in her essays and lectures. Local newspapers carry many pictures of Gloria Steinem, always in a happy "cluster" of women.

Before he died in 1980, Roland Barthes, the world-famous French sociologist and lexicologist, was suggesting in his Paris writings that women may be backing themselves into a *gynaeceum*. [23]

Gloria Steinem often dismisses men as expendable, and has deemed the institution of marriage "the only gamble most women take...or a way of reducing two people to one and a half." She has told classes of young women graduating from the universities: "We are becoming the men we once wanted to marry."

She also believes that "women grow more radical with age" — presumably with additional powers — as she prophesies that "one day an army of gray-haired women may quietly take over the earth." [24]

5
Women in the Workplace

It is unlikely that any country in the western world will ever again see a "Petticoat Strike" (as it was labelled by the press), such as occurred at Britain's largest disc brake factory in 1964, when 2,500 men of the Amalgamated Engineering Union went out on the streets because they feared a "petticoat" takeover at their plant — and were joined later by 500 women workers. Mr. Bryn Richards, a union official, declared: "This could be the thin edge of the wedge. With automation some firms might say that the whole factory could be run by women. But because automation makes a job easier, there is no reason to take it from a man who has sweated over it for years and give it to a woman."[1]

Today, we are told in surveys from the United Nations that women are now responsible for two-thirds of all labour undertaken throughout the world. In Canada, women comprise 43 per cent of the labour force, and are presently accounting for 65 per cent of the country's labour-force growth, with unemployment figures for women consistently lower than those for men — as much as one-quarter lower in the group of those under 24 years of age. Statistics Canada has also recorded that following the recession, the job recovery rate for full-time male employees was 36 per cent and for female employees 105 per cent.

Plainly, Canadian statistics indicate that women's numbers in the labour force will soon overtake those of men, and far surpass them by the turn of the century.[2]

(In the United States, the Bureau of Labor Statistics listed women as comprising 43 per cent of the American labour force by 1983, with the U.S. Labor Department predicting that two-thirds of all jobs created between then and the 1990s would be taken by women.)[3]

Of course, the flood of women into all spheres of the labour force is accelerated by the influence of women catapulted into managerial positions, as seen particularly in enforced government quotas (called by any other terms, they still amount to quotas).

Blatant examples of women elbowing hundreds of dedicated, able, and hardworking men aside, men with greater experience and seniority, are common in government programs. Federal Treasury Board Cabinet Minister Robert de Cotret has guaranteed that there will be 476 senior women managers by March 1988, in a program known as the "Double in Five Plan," introduced by former Treasury Board Minister Herb Gray who had promised to double the proportion of women managers every five years. Judy Erola, former Minister Responsible for the Status of Women, established the Women's Career Counselling Bureau to ensure the "Double in Five Plan." Operating nationwide, its continuing mandate is to counsel women who are two or three levels below senior management, as well as to attract other women from the private sector who might be interested in senior government posts. Department managers are ordered to identify women with management potential.

Within the first seven months of this program, 500 women were interviewed; forty of them were referred to the Public Service Commission's management category programs; eleven of these gained senior appointments immediately, while six others were given "development assignments," also called "bridging positions," which are usually new creations. [4]

As women already had 30 per cent of all managerial positions in the public sector by 1983, according to the figures published by Statistics Canada, the domination of women managers must soon become apparent. [5]

Indeed, in studying all the ramifications of the thousands of government-funded programs in Canada, steamrolling women past men at all levels, one must begin to wonder if men in the matriarchy will be allowed to have any work, any jobs except, perhaps, those considered most undesirable by the feminist dictators — such as homemaking and mining.

WOMEN IN THE UNIONS

Women's rise in leadership and numbers in Canadian unions in the past two decades has been considered phenomenal, but it is hardly surprising. By 1982, women were making up 32.3 per cent of all union membership in Canada, with their numbers increasing at double the rate of men's. By 1984, the Canadian Labour Congress (CLC), representing two million members, or more than 75 per cent of all union members in Canada, had created six vice-presidential positions for women, and elected women from across the country, under the CLC's new constitutional quota.

These women had already provided powerful voices for women in their own union — women such as Roxie Baker of the United Auto Workers, Stratford, Ontario; Louisette Hinton, of the United Food and Commercial

International Union, Quebec; and Frances Soboda, of the United Steelworkers of America, Nova Scotia. At the same time, the dynamic Shirley Carr, previously an executive vice-president of that national labour body, was acclaimed secretary-treasurer, the second highest office in the Congress, and only a short step from the presidency. In April 1986, she replaced Dennis McDermott as president, while Nancy Riche, formerly vice-president of the National Union of Provincial Government Employees, became one of the two executive vice-presidents.

Grace Hartman's name was to become a household word across Canada as she chalked up success after success as president of the Canadian Union of Public Employees (CUPE), the national union with the highest proportion of female employees (44 per cent by 1980). She has been credited with the growth of that civil service organization into the biggest and one of the most militant and effective unions on the continent, with such major achievements as the negotiation of the first pregnancy leave for part-time workers at the University of Toronto.

As more than 80 per cent of women working in Canada are employed in the gigantic service sector of the economy, a figure that remains constant, and more Canadians, almost 3.5 million, are employed in the service areas than any other (according to Statistics Canada), women's power becomes particularly apparent in such unions as the Ontario Public Service Employees' Union (OPSEU). The national Public Service Alliance (PSA) reports that women now make up more than 40 per cent of its total membership of 180,000.[6]

The proportion of female members of labour organizations is almost twice as high in Canada as in the United States, with Canadian women convinced that their solidarity in the unions is increasingly responsible for raising pay scales for men as well as for women. The minimum-wage laws won by the unions are recognized to have helped women more than men, but men also gained, as is usually the case in joint enterprises.[7]

However, women's particular issues have become a top priority in the aspirations and activities of many unions, with successes in one union lending impetus for the gearing up to battle in other unions. Since the Canadian Union of Postal Workers (CUPW) won pregnancy leave with 93 per cent of full salary for female workers, other unions have been inspired to campaign for similar benefits.[8]

Women's committees and caucuses organized by dynamic activists now abound throughout Canadian unions; their driving goal is to elect more women on union executives, guaranteeing their numbers on all negotiating boards. They have also demanded that their unions hire full-time staff responsible for special women's programs, and designate resources to implement these programs. CUPE and OPSEU are two of the major unions which have complied by providing staff devoted solely to women's interests.

Women are being sought out and encouraged to run for union leadership in union education courses, including stewards' training. The Steelworkers' Union offers specific scholarships to women in an effort to attract them to teaching positions, and by 1982, one-third of a group of new instructors in Ontario were women. Classes and local union meetings are usually scheduled to accommodate mothers, with child care or child care subsidies provided. Union literature advertises the fact that "parenthood has never been an impediment to men and will no longer be accepted as an impediment to women."[9]

The Confederation of Canadian Unions (CCU), a national labour conglomerate of twenty affiliated unions, representing 40,000 workers in diverse industries such as the Pulp, Paper and Woodworkers' Union in British Columbia, the Atlantic Oil Workers of Canada in Nova Scotia, and the York University Staff Association in

Ontario (which is 85 per cent female), certainly has been in the forefront of all the major battles for the rights of working women.

Sue Vohanka, writing in *Still Ain't Satisfied,* an anthology dealing with the progress of feminism, published in 1982, gives a comprehensive account of the CCU's influence as a participating member of the National Action Committee on the Status of Women, in which it "plays a leading role in developing NAC policies... and ensuring that these policies are pursued." The CCU claims that it was largely influential in having the Equal Pay for Work of Equal Value concept incorporated into the federal human rights legislation. In its union school workshops, strategies for political struggles are taught, as well as methods of achieving results at all the bargaining tables across the country.

Tirelessly, the CCU continues to campaign for universal child care; an additional two years' unpaid parental leave with accumulated seniority, following pregnancy leave with pay; and the same holiday, sick leave and pension benefits for part-time workers as for full-time workers.[10]

Then there are the independent all-female unions boasting that they are the best qualified to address the problems of the unorganized women workers across the country. Two of these, the Association of University and College Employees (AUCE), and the Service, Office and Retail Workers' Union of Canada (SORWUC), with head offices in Vancouver, have won some of the most outstanding clerical workers' first contracts. AUCE vanquished considerable opposition to establish a union at the University of British Columbia in 1972, and followed this success with the organization of unions at Simon Fraser University, the College of New Caledonia, and Notre Dame University.

The bulldog tenacity of SORWUC was admired by union members throughout Canada, when it took on the restaurant industry in Vancouver, maintaining picket lines at the Muckamuck Restaurant for over two years, overcoming injunctions and decertification attempts to win its battle. (Later, the restaurant went out of business.)[11]

Women have proven invaluable on the picket lines, particularly women with full-time working spouses, according to accusations in some management surveys. With all the women in the work force who are now sole breadwinners, this must be a generally unjust accusation. However, at the Glenna Carr rally in St. Catharines in April 1985, in support of workers seeking a first contract with the T. Eaton Company, one picketer told a reporter: "My husband has a good job — so if I lose this one I'm not going to suffer. I can stay out here for ever."

Rising militancy among feminist union members, which in many instances has been seen to surpass the men's, has long been recognized by male union members for its reciprocal advantages. So, it was not surprising that male and female union members would close ranks in the Ontario Federation of Labour which represents 800,000 workers, 300,000 of them women. President Cliff Pilkey joined vice-president Julie Griffen in a final effort to ensure Equal Pay for Work of Equal Value legislation for Ontario[12] in the spring of 1986.

While 62 per cent of all Canadian women work in what the feminists have named "the female ghettoes," secretarial, clerical, and service work, and seem to have no intention of giving up even one per cent of these to men, there are few formerly traditional male occupations that women have not coveted, moved into, or taken over, or are not planning to move into.

They have even mustered comparable physical strength and stamina, such as that required for firefighting. Karen Morrison, a former R.C.M.P. officer, now with the Windsor Fire Department, and Dianne Oland, previously a postal trucker and security guard, presently with the

Toronto Fire Department, both had to pass the strenuous physical tests for qualification. These included such feats as lifting ladders off trucks, walking obstacle courses blindfolded, and hauling eighty-five pounds of rubber hose up four stories, with the realization that lives would be depending on them.[13]

Of course, there are hundreds of government-funded programs teaching women all the skills they will need in various trades, with special medically supervised fitness classes provided to increase their physical prowess. One leading example is Skiltec, established in 1983 in North Bay, Ontario, to encourage women to become welders or sheet-metal workers.[14]

All barriers to women in the trades have been swept aside, under government directives and legislation, although accommodating women in the trades often proves costly. One master plumber (with government contracts) complained that a female apprentice had walked off a job suddenly at five o'clock to pick up her children at the babysitter's — leaving him with an impossible situation involving burst pipes and no helper. Today, his company will not accept a job on which they must use female plumbers or apprentices, unless they can estimate the completion of the job by three or four o'clock.

Sometimes accommodating women has raised insurmountable problems, such as one that faced Inco, following the hiring of women in its Sudbury nickel refinery in 1974. In 1975, the medical director, Dr. Ken Hedges, instituted a policy forbidding women of childbearing age to work in areas where they might be exposed to certain chemicals that had not been cleared for teratogenicity (ability to cause birth defects).

Combatting the feminist furore that usually ensues, management in numerous companies across Canada and throughout the United States pay lawyers millions of dollars to argue that their decisions are not intended to be discriminatory, that "women just happened to have the bad luck to be the vehicles for carrying future generations."[15]

Many of these companies have simply been unable to meet feminist demands to redesign whole plants, change whole industries or systems in order to safeguard the fetus, which is known to be more susceptible to dangers in the workplace than the adult man or woman.

There is little doubt that Canadian feminist union leaders, as they achieve more and more concessions and benefits for women throughout Canadian industry, will continue to force wages up generally, far above the comparative scale in American industry. Paul Kovacs, the Canadian Manufacturers' Association's chief economist, in an article dealing with the effects of the Equal Pay for Work of Equal Value legislation, stated: "We already have one of the highest wage costs in the world."[16] That Canadian wages must sometimes adjust to the American scale certainly became a principal target of union resistance to the Canada-United States free trade negotiations.

Nevertheless, some high-profile union leaders throughout the provinces, particularly in the west, seem to be looking far beyond such adjustments to a more secure future, in co-operation with the country's largest trading partner.

WOMEN IN MANAGEMENT — THE FEMINIZED ECONOMY

If anyone ever doubted women's executive abilities, they would only have to examine the superstructure of power the feminists in the Canadian Women's Liberation Movement are building or have built into every department of government, federal, provincial, and municipal, across the country, to be enlightened. The 1970 federal Royal Commission on the Status of Women laid the foundations, and since then, the thousands of government-funded agencies devoted to women's advantages and advancement in every area have been a dominant force in Canadian politics and society.

Moving women rapidly into management, for the purpose of snowballing more women into high positions, has been a very successful building principle. Encouraging and coddling women of all ages past all barriers, such as training, experience, and seniority has become a common practice, called "bridging." Clerks, secretaries, and receptionists have told their stories of being "pushed" by affirmative action personnel and programs into the "bridging" positions — positions often created or contrived in which they might quickly acquire new administrative skills.

There have been 1,500 such "bridging" jobs designed to accelerate women to become managers in the Ontario legislature alone — where a superstructure becomes a model. There is also a special fund for ministries to draw on, when they wish to go over budget in giving women promotions. All ministries have affirmative action managers with mandates to seek out promotable women using programs involving workshops, films, and seminars.

In 1985 the ministries were reprimanded for failing to fill forty-seven jobs targeted for women, due to a lack of qualified women applicants. However, that situation will be corrected by a search for more female applicants in the private sector. (I have been told that never for a moment did anyone consider giving any of those jobs to men.)

The Ontario Women's Directorate, with an $8 million budget and a permanent staff of fifty-one, is solely concerned with women's interests, especially the monitoring of the progress of affirmative action in all ministries. Women presently comprise more than 30 per cent of all managers, but this figure is expected to rise dramatically under the leadership of Glenna Carr, head of the OWD, and such affirmative action managers as Sherry Baker (formerly an Ontario Provincial Police constable), in the Office of the Solicitor-General.

Pushing men aside sometimes constitutes a struggle, nevertheless, according to Ms. Carr. "There are dinosaurs who still think the world is like it was twenty-five years ago," she lamented, in a *Globe and Mail* article.[17]

Derision and contempt seem to be lethal weapons in the hands of powerful media feminists in the Canadian Women's Liberation revolution, with "dinosaurs" the most common and disparaging epithet. "Women Send Messages to Television Dinosaurs," heads a Doris Anderson article in *The Toronto Star*, March 8, 1986. Politicians slow to acquiesce to feminists' demands are described as "dodos," in an article in *Chatelaine*, January 1985. Columnist Sam Ion discusses "the old fogeys with outdated ideas," in *The Toronto Sun*, March 21, 1986. Then there is Betty Friedan speaking of "dreary housewives" to Harry Brown on TV Ontario's program, *Speaking Out*, March 6, 1986.

Of course, there are all the marvellously motivated and dedicated women who are still rising through the ranks to the top, without any need of feminist springboards or ladders, as surely as a Margaret Thatcher, or a Mary Isobel MacDonald (the famous Vancouver stockbroker, who died recently at 83, and is particularly remembered as Canada's top seller of War Bonds during the 1940s).

Today, Jean Boyd, the powerful, able, and immensely popular superintendent of the Metro Toronto Police Force, is also such a woman. A 49-year-old Scottish immigrant, single and with a great singleness of purpose, she is in full charge of all hiring, training, and career development on the Force. However, an important part of her mandate is to increase the number of women officers, as recommended by feminist lobbies.[18]

It would appear that women actually have a particular aptitude and talent for management in police work, as was illustrated in March 1985, when Kingston Penitentiary Warden Mary Dawson brought a most serious hostage-taking incident to a conclusion. Furthermore, it is predicted that more and more women will take over other administrative positions in all related police and penitentiary fields, as special funds ensure female recruitment, and women in all the lower echelons are attracted to senior posts. In 1984 in Regina, the Royal Canadian Mounted Police listed twenty-four women of the thirty-eight trainees, and if this proportion continued, it would only be a matter of time before female members dominate in Canada's illustrious national police force.

While women continue blithely to leapfrog over men to attain management positions in all areas of government throughout Canada, helped by affirmative action programs, they have had to engage in more "warrior-type" tactics to reach the same heights in the private sector. However, it has also been shown in numerous surveys that male business leaders have found themselves disarmed and beating a retreat, justified or otherwise, almost as often as the male politicians under feminist attacks.

Earle McLaughlin, chairman of the Royal Bank of Canada in 1976, was mowed down by feminist fury, after he issued a statement that the bank had been unable to find a qualified woman to serve on its board of directors (after all, 40 per cent of all bank employees are women). Two months later, Mitzi Dobrin, daughter of Sam Steinberg, and executive vice-president of Steinberg, Inc. of Montreal, was named a director. Yet, the following year, she corroborated Mr. McLaughlin's statement. "It's not easy to find a woman. . . . I know because I'm now on the nominating committee at the Royal Bank. If a woman's name comes up, there are hundreds of boards after her," she declared.[19]

The private sector was learning its lesson, and ten years later, there may not be a company in Canada without its rapidly growing list of women board members, as indicated in recent publications of the Conference Board of Canada.

Nor is it likely that many companies in Canada would dare to promote or hire a man to fill a managerial position if *any* woman was applying. If they did, they might find themselves besieged, in a veritable hornet's nest, an experience suffered by the Toronto City Council when members elected a man as their City Solicitor, rather than a lone female applicant, and then had to spend a week cowering from the press, while they tried to explain that they truly believed that the man had the best qualifications. The Metro Toronto Council was seen to have a better record, with the feminists lauding such appointments as that of Carol Ruddell as the influential general manager of the Metro Licensing Commission.

There are no longer any male strongholds. Even the giant 70-year-old Big Brothers organization of Metro Toronto, seeking a new executive director, with thirteen qualifying applicants from across the country and only two of them women, did not hesitate in appointing one of the two women, Barbara Hickey.[20] In another field, still surprisingly male-dominated, Claudette MacKay-Lassonde, described as a tough-minded feminist, became president of the Professional Engineers of Ontario.[21]

Meg Mitchell of the prestigious executive search firm, The Thomas-Mitchell Associates, was admitting by 1984 that over 65 per cent of all her firm's placements in Canadian corporations as well as in governments were women.

The pressures applied by governments to the private sector to ensure the rise of women to management even prior to the binding, punitive affirmative action legislation, have been significant, as evident in the "consulting" services of the Canadian Employment and Immigration Commission. CEIC is staffed by 22,000 people, 57 per cent of whom are women. By 1984, sixty-five prominent companies in the private sector had submitted to affirmative action guidelines under a CEIC Workforce Audit and Systems Analysis.[22]

WOMEN IN ADVERTISING

Corporate "head-hunters" seeking out women have been seen as instrumental in swelling the numbers of women taking over executive posts throughout American and Canadian advertising. Major Canadian agencies point with pride to their women executives of the calibre of Wendy Stratten, senior vice-president of Ted Bates Advertising, Inc., at the Toronto office, and Madeleine Saint-Jacques, senior vice-president and managing director of Young & Rubicam Ltd., in Montreal.

Barrie Wilson, vice-president and education director of the Institute of Canadian Advertisers (ICA), representing sixty-six of Canada's largest agencies, has prophesied that women will definitely dominate the advertising industry in the near future, as they already outnumber their male counterparts in many key areas. In 1985, women comprised 68 per cent of the total enrolment of the ICA's Certified Advertising Practitioner Program.[23]

No one underestimates the power of advertising, and feminist power in Canadian advertising may prove an ultimate weapon in ensuring a matriarchy — power from inside and from outside the industry. Feminists are already clearly controlling advertising, with their persistent pressure on government regulatory bodies such as the Canadian Radio-Television and Telecommunications Commission (CRTC).

No more "doting, stay-at-home mothers" or "dippy housewives in the Ring-Around-The-Collar advertisements" are to be tolerated (although Alan Rae, president of Lever Detergents in Canada, showed reluctance at giving up an immensely lucrative campaign, "because some raving feminists have complained.") Since then, however, President Rae has done a turnabout, as chairman of the

Advertising Advisory Board (AAB) sub-committee on sex-stereotyping.

Projecting their own image in advertising is obviously the feminists' goal. Judith Posner, sociology professor at Toronto's York University and a board member of Media-Watch, a nationwide activist group, denounces the advertisement of the executive woman "with the attache case and Harry Rosen suit... still head-cocking at the boardroom table... being blatantly seductive." At the same time there has been no disapproval noted of the Mappins advertisement of a similar tailored business woman, smoking a huge cigar, displaying large pieces of jewellery, with the slogan, "You're Worth Mappins."

Other jewellery advertisements of the 1985 and 1986 seasons depict women buying jewellery for the men in their lives.[24] One must wonder if many of these advertisements are sex-stereotyping in reverse — such as that very appealing television commercial of a father and the children waving from a window as the mother hurries away down the front path.

Advertising aimed directly at women is sometimes even more radically untraditional. For instance, an extensive campaign for condoms in the United States is aimed exclusively at the female market, at points of sale and in women's magazines, as well as in the packaging. An article in *Working Woman*, October 1985, claimed that "women make up about 40 per cent of the consumers tossing condoms into shopping carts."

WOMEN IN COMMUNICATIONS

Feminist power is probably the greatest and most insidious force in communications — television, radio, magazines, and newspapers. However, it is absolutely impossible to obtain statistics on the male-female ratios involved from any Canadian television or radio network or publication. One male executive explained: "Why should we expose any of our figures, voluntarily — when we know that if we are only a few percentage points under in the female ratio, we risk feminist investigation, and persecution, and constraints, through various government agencies."

However, statistics recording female involvement and control in all areas of communications have been available in the United States for several years. In 1975, the Columbia University Press published an authoritative book, *The Female of the Species*, by M. Kay Martin and Barbara Voorhies, that stated: "Women have come to so monopolize positions in the vast communications networks of this nation that a joint strike for a single day would virtually paralyze the American economy" (p. 399).

WOMEN IN SALES AND MARKETING

Women crowding out men, taking over the lead, and moving to the top in sales and marketing is not an unusual scenario in the Eighties. Female numbers have more than doubled in brokerage firms, and have tripled in business services, insurance, and real estate in the past decade in Canada, according to census figures.

When the U.S. magazine, *Working Woman*, in a 1985 spring issue, asked seventy-three female executives to suggest a woman's easiest route to the top, the consensus pointed to sales and marketing. Now Canadian companies have recruiting campaigns underway on all university campuses, seeking women for this field.

Women have long been credited with particular aptitude and skills in residential real estate, and are presently outdistancing men in ever-increasing numbers. Yoki Nichol of Calgary was one such woman featured in a *Financial Post Magazine* article, as outearning "99 per cent of Royal LePage's nearly 7,000 residential realtors nationwide," with her annual income estimated "between $120,000 and $140,000." Royal LePage also acknowledged that with only 56 per cent of its sales force female,

70 per cent of its award-winners in 1984 were women.

The magazine article featured other female sales "stars" throughout Canadian industry, documenting their dedication to their careers. Yoki Nichol refused to move when her common-law husband was lured to a Toronto job, opting instead for a long-distance relationship. Some featured women were single. Kajhilda Grant, a 36-year-old single, and a former clerk, became Xerox's leading Canadian salesperson in 1980, with an income then reported as $128,000; Bonnie Isbister, 44 and single, began selling to bars, hotels, and liquor stores in downtown Toronto in 1976, but by 1979, she had won Seagram's Wall of Excellence Award, as that company's top salesperson in Canada; Connie Festa, 33, perhaps the typical "born businesswoman," who began her career as a keypunch operator, had only been with ICL Computers Ltée in Montreal for two years when she received the company's "Above and Beyond Award for Achievement," accompanied by a trip to Switzerland. Wed at 19, she would see her marriage dissolve as she moved into management.

It is astonishing that *The Financial Post Magazine* was not attacked by the feminists for its "sexist" suggestion in the article that women's aptitude for selling might be attributed to their "attentiveness.... Raised to be nurturers, they excel at meeting clients' needs — and at sensing those needs in the first place."[25]

Actually, "singleness of purpose" has been the one predominant characteristic cited in most studies of corporate female executives. A survey undertaken by the University of California, Los Angeles, and Korn-Ferry International, a consulting firm, involving 300 women financial officers, vice-presidents, senior managers and lawyers, all drawn from the Fortune 500 Industry and Service lists, was to find that more than 50 per cent of them were unmarried, and 61 per cent had no children. Some of these women would willingly admit that they

had deliberately traded all family considerations for the
panelled boardroom and its accompanying power, prestige,
and money.[26]

Still, many of them would find bonuses in office
romances, according to Scott de Garmo, editor of
Success Magazine. On a *Today Morning Television* program, he and Eliza Collins of *The Harvard Business
Review* discussed surveys that indicated that 50 per cent
of all American female executives were having office
affairs. Their concern was with the ensuing problem of
which one should leave the company when the relationship was terminated.[27]

MONEY

Remuneration for women executives is often greater
now than for their male counterparts, and may continue
to climb higher, according to American economists, who
foresee feminist power in the setting of wage scales. A
national newspaper, *USA Today,* carried a front-page
story in December 1985, dealing with a reversal in the
traditional salary gap in some formerly male-dominated
fields. Women petroleum engineers, agricultural and
food scientists, and law professors were among those
reported to be earning up to 25 per cent more than men
in comparable positions. Furthermore, university studies
confirm the fact that two-thirds of the women currently
entering the labour force at all levels are choosing
traditionally male occupations.

A United States Census Bureau publication has indicated that by 1984 there were already six million women
throughout the United States earning considerably more
than their husbands.

SMALL BUSINESS

A spectacular trend in the "feminizing" of the economy

in Canada has been seen in the entrepreneurial success of thousands of Canadian women who have begun their own businesses during the past ten years. With the number of self-employed women increasing five times faster than the number of self-employed men, by 1979 the number of small businesses owned by women in Canada had risen to 36 per cent of all firms, and by 1985, was nearing 50 per cent.

There are now numerous Canadian and American economists across the continent who are predicting that by the year 2000, women will visibly dominate the business world — as owners or managers of the majority of small companies, while others are running the majority of the larger corporations.

Helen Bullock, a *Toronto Star* columnist, whose balancing of views in an unbalanced society I never cease to admire, speaks for many when she writes: "Exactly what role men will play in this Amazonian corporate culture is anybody's guess."[28]

6
Feminist Power in Politics and Legislation

Marxism, particularly as systematized in the writings of Friedrich Engels, has certainly been influential in the Women's Liberation Movement throughout the United States and Canada. In 1884, thirty-six years after the publication of *The Communist Manifesto*, Engels wrote: "The emancipation of women becomes possible only when women are enabled to take part in production on a large, social scale, and when domestic duties require their attention only to a minor degree."[1] Lenin himself stated: "Unless women are brought to take an independent part not only in political life generally, but also in daily and universal public service, it is no use talking about... socialism."[2]

Women were subjected to a so-called liberation in Russia, banished from their homes to street-cleaning, mining, and factory work, as well as to engineering, law, and medicine. Ninety-one per cent of all doctors in Russia are now female. However, it is surprising to observe Russian women today being attracted back to a former femininity, with increasing revenues allowed for women's clothing and cosmetics, while theatre and fiction are beginning specifically to honour the domestic mother-homemaker. Actually, this trend began after World War II, with the loss of almost half of Russia's male population, and the launching of many incentives to encourage marriage and childbearing, and, of course, the birth rate continues to be a major Soviet concern.

In the western world in the past two decades feminists have been conducting their own revolutionary upheaval of traditional society while demanding state support of a type definitely in line with communist principles, as in state-funded day care.

Finance Minister Michael Wilson was severely criticized by Marjorie Cohen, vice-president of the National Action Committee on the Status of Women for failing to address the need for a universal day care program in the February 1986 budget. He could report back to her that a Conservative committee had already begun a national study on child care, according to NAC wishes, while the findings of a Liberal-appointed task force studying the subject would be published.[3]

In that same budget, the Finance Minister announced that the government would provide "$800 million for retraining women re-entering the work force, and for young people."[4]

In March 1986, the Canadian Press reported that the Minister's Office was setting up yet another special advisory agency, this time to ensure that 50 per cent of all government appointments to federal boards, commissions, courts and government posts be given to women,[5] again ignoring seniority, experience, and the specific qualifications that any male applicant might offer.

That same week, the lesbian faction of the National Action Committee on the Status of Women was rewarded when the federal government addressed a major resolution that was passed at NAC's last annual meeting, demanding lesbian rights. The federal Justice Minister, John Crosbie, announced the introduction of a law that forbids any discrimination based on sexual orientation, in all areas under federal jurisdiction.[6]

AFFIRMATIVE ACTION
AND EQUAL PAY

Women are rapidly moving into all areas, and reaching all levels of government.

Unlike their American counterparts, some Canadian male politicians are gracefully stepping aside. Donald Johnson, a candidate in the 1984 Liberal leadership race, told 300 delegates at an all-candidates' meeting dealing with party reform, that the only way to put a lot more women in Parliament was to "get more men out." This could be achieved if elected Members of Parliament voluntarily limited their terms in office. He had personally pledged to stay in politics for only ten years when he came to Ottawa, but, he said, if he was elected leader, he would extend the time. But "not by very much," he promised — to the prolonged applause of feminist groups.[7]

The Canadian Human Rights Institute, comprising 300 members across Canada, among them senators, judges, and lawyers, charged with the study of the equality rights section under the Charter of Rights and Freedoms, recommended that the government act "for whatever time the Senate exists... to make the Senate clearly representative of both halves of the population and therefore to democratize the Upper House of Parliament."

Former Senator Eugene Forsey, Canada's foremost expert on constitutional affairs, seems to have raised the only dissenting voice on this directive, suggesting that "imposing quotas by sex is altogether foolish, in that every individual appointment should be based on the candidate's abilities, with all variables considered."[8]

It is interesting to note that all Canadians between the ages of 30 and 75 who have a residence in Canada and own property worth at least $4,000 are eligible to become senators — *and that more women than men are eligible for these appointments.* The number of women is 5.3 million, exceeding the number of men at 5.1 million. (The late Toronto broadcaster, Gordon Sinclair, is remembered for repeatedly telling women to stop whining about all their disadvantages, as they always had more homes, property, and money than the men, and sometimes he would offer enlightening statistics.)

Feminists could expect all their causes to be further promoted when Walter McLean, Secretary of State and federal Minister Responsible for the Status of Women, appointed Kay Stanley as his full-time political advisor on women's issues. A former schoolteacher, she is known to be committed to the greater involvement of women in all senior levels of government, on influential federal task forces, all boards and tribunals, as well as in the training programs that will accelerate their advancement.

"The Minister has offered me the opportunity to do everything in my power to sustain and enhance the momentum achieved so far by Canadian women," Kay Stanley exulted. "Now is the time for us to work *on the inside* [my italics] to help influence changes at the centre, where so many crucial decisions are taken that affect our daily lives."[9]

Working *on the inside* is fast becoming the name of the game in the Canadian Women's Liberation Movement, although there would appear to be few radical feminists among the present women cabinet ministers and other members of Parliament. Most of them are women from across the country who have exceptional qualities and abilities, with wide experience in leadership that preceded the Women's Liberation Movement in Canada. Biographical studies have shown that there was no leapfrogging for these women, nor any other boosts up those feminist ladders. Nor would feminist influence seem to be a factor in certain government appointments, such as that of the brilliant Judith Maxwell, recently named chairman of the Economic Council of Canada, who was not dropped into that authoritative economic body from the quota system.

Still, there are thousands of feminists now in the federal and provincial governments from coast to coast, who have arrived in strategic positions through affirmative action directives, many of them endorsing Kay Stanley's aspirations of increasing "the momentum" of women moving into all areas of government. Some of them are very visible and vocal, while others, quietly, with subtle determination and considerable powers, definitely influence legislation.

For example, eight months into her job as president of the Canadian Advisory Council on the Status of Women, Sylvia Gold was predicting a "renewal of militancy" in the Council. In her prestigious position that pays between $56,640 and $66,000 a year, she has the constant ear of the Secretary of State, Walter McLean, in bi-monthly meetings devoted solely to women's interests, such as economic opportunities, pensions, job security and child care.[10]

The Council, with a $2.4 million budget, is backed by the Office of the Co-ordinator of the Status of Women, a federal agency that ensures that all new federal bills, policies, and programs are considered in light of their impact on women. Furthermore, this is the only office with access to all Cabinet documents.[11]

The power of such women as Elinor Caplan in the Ontario provincial government to effect change in favour of women is plain to see. A first-time member of the house and cabinet minister, she was appointed chairman of the new Ontario Liberal cabinet in 1985, where she refereed all key decisions. She was also chairman of the management board, wielding enormous influence in every facet of government spending. Furthermore, as Minister of Government Services, she was recognized as the corporate chief of all government business, while as head of the civil service commission she employed 80,000 public service workers.

She became known as a powerful feminist champion while chairman of the Women's Perspective Advisory Committee that reported to Premier David Peterson when he was leader of the Ontario opposition party. She was described in the press then as the "powerhouse personality of the backroom group of tough-minded women,"[12] and in her new commanding positions, she claimed headlines, jostling an admiring Premier off the front pages. The only other cabinet minister with as much power and responsibility was said to be the veteran politician, Treasurer Robert Nixon, former leader of the Liberal Party in Ontario.

Elinor Caplan's meteoric rise has not been astonishing in a feminist world, nor is the prediction that she could be a mighty contender for future Liberal leadership, either provincially or federally. After finishing high school, she married at 19, raised four children, and graduated from volunteer work (such as a stint as chairman of Toronto's Hadassah Bazaar), to local school boards, ratepayers' groups, and finally political riding associations. An extremely hard worker, she lost no time in instituting feminist directives in the new Liberal government's legislation.

"Technically, as employer of the government," she said, "my job is to implement Pay Equity [Equal Pay for Work of Equal Value] in the civil service.... I've had great input into its formulation."[13]

There was great consternation in government ranks when this able woman was forced to relinquish her cabinet appointments due to suggested conflict of interest in family-related affairs.

No one was surprised when the new Ontario Attorney-

General Ian Scott, referred to the Women's Liberation Movement as "one of the significant revolutions of this century," or when *The Globe and Mail* in Toronto reported that "Equal Value legislation is at the top of Mr. Scott's priorities, and is clearly the program on which the minister plans to hang his reputation in the women's portfolio."[14]

Within three and a half months after the Liberals took office in Ontario, he was also promising "$1 million for fighting equality cases under the Charter of Rights and Freedoms, the removal from the Human Rights Code of a section that barred women from men's sports teams, and a $300,000 education program to encourage women to start their own businesses."[15]

He does hesitate to promise child care legislation, as "to be frank, there is no way any government can meet the child care needs of this province in the short term, without sort of tripling the income tax," he explained.[16]

Meanwhile, women of influence multiply, week by week, on the federal scene, appearing in all departments of government in increasing numbers. Feminists particularly lauded the appointment of Janet Smith as the Associate Deputy Minister of Transport. Formerly she was with the Privy Council Office as an assistant to the Cabinet on economic matters. She was a Director-General of the Anti-Inflation Board from 1977 to 1979, but had also become well known as the co-ordinator in the Office of Equal Opportunity for Women in the Public Service Commission from 1972 to 1974. She now acts as co-ordinator between the Department of Transport and other central agencies, such as the Treasury Board, and is involved in the development of policies and programs, as a consultant dealing with the Department's Crown corporations, such as Via Rail.[17]

Party politics may naturally fall into feminist patterns, led by national Liberal Party president Iona Campagnolo, and New Democratic Party president Marion Dewar, former mayor of Ottawa. It is estimated that 90 per cent of all election campaign workers in the United States and Canada are women. Female candidates are being sought and groomed to run in all constituencies. With increasing numbers of female delegates ensured from across Canada, it could be only a few years before women come to dominate the electorate from the grass roots.

There were men and women who asked if there was an extraordinary miscarriage of justice when the former federal Minister of Employment and Immigration, Lloyd Axworthy, appointed 38-year-old Ontario Provincial Court Judge Rosalie Abella as the sole member of the Royal Commission on Equality of Employment, rather than several members — men and women — as the study will undoubtedly affect the lives of every man, woman, and child in the country.

Judge Abella's report, tabled November 20, 1985, after a 16-month study of eleven Crown and government-owned corporations and agencies (such as Air Canada and the Canadian Broadcasting Corporation), brought forth 117 recommendations, mainly dealing with the concerns of feminists, and couched in feminist rhetoric. The whole thrust of the report was toward legislation enforcing measures for the advancement of women, which "is permissible under the Charter of Rights and Freedoms" (Section 15).[18]

"Equality demands enforcement. It is not enough to be able to claim equal rights," she has insisted, speaking to various women's groups. Legal remedies, called "intervention to adjust the system," laws enforcing affirmative action, and pay equity would remove the barriers to women's progress:

> Employment equity would revise the role women play in the work force. It would mean they would be taken seriously as workers instead of facing the view that their role is in the home . . . their changing role in the care of the family would be recognized, and

= Marxist-Leninist

this would help them and their male *husbands* ? partners to both have jobs and share the role of parenting. . . . Employment equity would mean providing the education and training to allow women the chance to compete for any job they want.[19]

While the directives were for federal legislation, Judge Abella recommended that all provincial governments enact similar laws. She is said to have coined the term "employment equity," but her use of the term "pay equity" in place of "equal pay for work of equal value," has been called cunningly misleading — as all the provinces have had "pay equity" laws — equal pay for equal work — for some time. (In England it was on the Trade Union Agenda in 1888.)

EQUAL PAY FOR WORK OF EQUAL VALUE

In the United States, Congress passed the Equal Pay Act in 1963, prior to the onslaught of the Women's Liberation Revolution, and all states have been enforcing the law, to the letter, since then. However, the present principal demand of the American and Canadian Women's Liberation Movement, for "Equal Pay for Work of Equal Value," has been successfully denied, year after year, by American legislators, while Canadian legislators, federal and provincial, seem blissfully prepared to follow Judge Rosalie Abella's directives.

As Deputy Minister of Labour, Jennifer McQueen, 54, a career public servant, has been charged with specific responsibilities in implementing equality measures in the Abella Report, at the federal level. Formerly a commissioner in the federal public service, she became known for her influence and expertise in encouraging and placing women in middle management and executive positions. Another key appointment by the Conservative government was that of Linda Geller-Schwartz, 37, as Director-General of the Women's Bureau. A former head of the Labour Department's Part-Time Employ-ment Unit, undoubtedly she will now be called on by feminist activists to further all feminist goals in govern-ment, such as Equal Pay for Work of Equal Value.[20]

The most prominent American economists have consistently spoken out against a policy that they see as a snare and a delusion. June O'Neil, of the Urban Insti-tute, a Washington think tank, argues that the policy would lead to "repealing supply and demand in the marketplace," and would result in "radical distortions of the economy."[21]

Another powerful voice, among thousands, has been that of Clarence M. Pendleton, Jr., Chairman of the United States Commission on Civil Rights, who said Congress would need a "tooth fairy" to pay "the $320 billion a year cost if a national comparable-worth policy became law." At the same time, the United States Chamber of Commerce announced "that in addition to the cost, the inflation rate would rise to a minimum of 9.7 per cent — from 4 per cent," scuppering the current economic recovery.[22]

In Canada, two alarming headlines appeared in *The Toronto Star*, February 12, 1986: "Equal Pay Law to Cost Ontario $88 Million a Year," and "Equal Pay Bill Would Boost Some Wages by $3,000." These were followed on February 13 by a *Star* editorial stating:

> Equal Pay for Work of Equal Value or Pay Equity, as it is now being called, is a fuzzy concept... we have opposed the concept and urged the provincial gov-ernment to consider other programs....
>
> But the Liberal government, bound as it is by its accord last June with the New Democratic Party, seems determined to adopt the concept, at least for

its own employees (in its civil service of 75,000 members). We urge the government to stop there for now
and not impose Pay Equity on other public-sector
employees, such as municipalities and school boards,
or on the private sector.... It is one thing for the
government to accept that price and to lay it off on
the taxpayer. It is another thing entirely for a
private-sector employer who would have to get the
money from somewhere else.

Morley Gunderson, a University of Toronto industrial
economist, in his analysis, *Costing Equal Value in Ontario*,
estimates the cost between $1 billion and $6 billion, and
believes it will certainly reduce Ontario firms' ability to
compete in world markets, lessen Ontario's appeal to all
investors, and increase the numbers of business failures,
while many companies will make haste to relocate outside
the province.

A suggested point system to fix pay levels may take into
account nine factors, as in the Aiken Plan, developed in
1946. They are as follows: the complexity of the job;
education; experience; initiative; physical and mental
demands; the effect job errors would have; the relative
importance of contacts within the company; the nature
of supervision required; and working conditions.[23]

"Different Job Skills and Conditions Can't be Distilled
into a Formula," flatly announced a headline of an article
in *Newsweek* by Robert J. Samuelson.

Your pay reflects luck, skill, the supply and demand
for different jobs, whether or not you work for a
profitable firm or in a profitable industry or whether
you belong to a union.... Most companies pay what
they must.... This patchwork pay system may not
be fair, but it produces jobs because it is flexible and
can adjust to changing circumstances. Comparable

worth threatens this flexibility and diversity; wage setting would become more rigid, formal and prone to second-guessing — and lawsuits. [24]

John Crispo, Professor of Political Economy in the Faculty of Management Studies at the University of Toronto, has been warning national legislators:

> Equal Pay for Work of Equal Value will require an army of job evaluators to assess the relative worth of virtually every kind of job in the country. Ultimately, this could lead to a nightmarish bureaucracy presiding over a highly arbitrary national job-evaluation system based on a host of equally highly subjective criteria. [25]

Meanwhile, the authoritative Fraser Institute's publication, *Discrimination, Affirmative Action, and Equal Opportunity*, pointed out the fact that in the United States, "single women with a commitment to the labor force earn, on average, more than single men." The Fraser Institute's 1982 report, which confirmed that the earnings of single women in Canada were 99 per cent of those of single men with comparable commitment to their jobs, has been largely ignored. [26]

Leading economists in the country are employed by our "Think Tanks," as well as by our national newspapers and magazines, but Canadian legislators in charge of the economy have apparently stopped paying any attention to them.

"In Canada, the women's movement has managed to get a stranglehold on our policy-makers," Barbara Amiel, a *Maclean's* columnist and *Toronto Sun* editor, was writing by 1984. "If it succeeds in opening the doors of state interference and in the denial of reality in order to fit everything into its members' warped ideological mould, it will wreak havoc with the lives of us all — men, women and children."[27]

Richard Gwyn, author, television interviewer, and respected *Toronto Star* columnist, was also writing authoritative articles on the Canadian economy "becoming feminized" by 1984.[28]

REVERSE DISCRIMINATION

Orland French, daily columnist in *The Globe and Mail*, offered a scorching condemnation of reverse discrimination in the new Ontario pay equity law "the new jargon for Equal Pay for Work of Equal Value," wondering, "when laws against discrimination are themselves inherently discriminatory... how society is being better served." The "government-sanctioned discrimination" against men, of course, was built into the Charter of Rights, "which was designed with a hole in it... Subsection 15(2)... to allow governments to discriminate."[29]

In the United States, a federal Court of Appeal overturned an earlier court decision that would have forced the State of Washington to eliminate a 20 per cent wage difference between male truck drivers and female clerk-typists; and other wage differences such as those of male campus police and female secretaries, and male computer-analysts and female nurses — implementation of which had been estimated between $330 million and $1 billion, and might have caused bankruptcy for the State.[30]

At the same time, the Canadian federal Court of Appeal upheld a Canadian Human Rights Commission ruling that Canadian National (CN) must hire one woman employee in every four for all blue-collar openings in its affirmative action program. Former Canadian National chairman Betty Hewes and President Maurice LeClair demonstrated that with women applicants failing mechanical aptitude tests, and physically unable to handle the required weights and welding, the company would simply have to let that fourth female "sit in a corner."

Ignoring the differences in physical prowess of men and women is considered madness among the opponents of reverse discrimination through wage equity and affirmative action programs. Furthermore, there are numerous studies, such as those undertaken by the American government's Pay Equity Committee, that indicate that the largest percentage of women across the continent do not ignore them either, but consistently gravitate to work with fewer physical demands, as in offices and stores. With pleasant working conditions and relatively short hours, these jobs offer more flexibility as well, to accommodate home and other outside interests.[31]

These jobs are in the "female ghettoes," according to the feminists, who are determined to "get women out of them," often against their will. It is the Women's Liberation Movement's dictatorship in action. As they fail to move many of these women, they will, nevertheless, have them paid the same wages as the men in all their tougher, more demanding occupations.

Denying biology has always been a linchpin in the Women's Liberation Movement. However, more and more biological evidence that there are mental and emotional, as well as physical constraints on women's performance in the workplace, that should be considered in Equal Pay for Work of Equal Value and affirmative action decisions, is now being published.

Conclusive American studies show that women are ill more often than men, although absentee lists are still suppressed in Canada. Premenstrual Syndrome, PMS, has been recognized as a "true" disease by the American Medical Association, affecting up to 40 per cent of all women between the ages of 30 and 40. According to Dr. Karen Owens, Professor of Nutritional Biochemistry at the University of Minnesota, symptoms include nervous tension, irritability, mood changes, crying, insomnia, forgetfulness, confusion, and in extreme cases, suicidal depression. Physical effects may be weight gain, dizziness, headaches, abdominal swelling, and joint pains. Toronto doctor Diane McGibbon, speaking on *Canada AM*, a CTV production, explained that any of these symptoms could last from four to fourteen days.

Menopausal problems are also a fact of female biology as the case of former Chicago mayor Jane M. Byrne (nicknamed "Hot-Flash Jane"), who was accused of being "menopausally unhinged," when she came under the scrutiny of a state grand jury for allegedly mishandling state funds. [32]

There are still those women who are not troubled by PMS, as well as the exceptional women who are able to cope with female physical deterrents at all ages, without missing a beat in their performance in the workplace. Feminists point to women of the calibre of Libby Riddles, 1985 winner of the world's most famous dog-sled race, a gruelling test of strength for men and women over mountain ranges along the Yukon River; the Newfoundland women training to ski to the North Pole across an unconquered transpolar drift; Sharon Wood, the 28-year-old mountain guide from Alberta, one of the eleven members of a Canadian climber expedition attempting to scale Mount Everest; and the female truck drivers hoisting their cargoes from coast to coast. However, if such women are unusual, and not in the majority, how can legislators equate the capabilities of all women with those of men in the Equal Pay for Work of Equal Value and affirmative action programs?

Of course, feminists have rushed forward with statistics on the higher rate of heart attacks among men. Those differences in rates between men and women are now narrowing significantly as women in corporate fields fall under the same pressures as men.

American opponents to reverse discrimination have published statistics that consistently show that women come and go in the workplace. "It is not usual for men to leave their jobs to have children, and they are less likely than women to leave their jobs to care for children. They are less likely to move if their spouses are forced to relocate for professional purposes," one study emphasizes.

Another important consideration is highlighted in a study based on the United States Department of Labor statistics, "estimating that the number of years men stay on their jobs exceeds that for women by 77 to 100 per cent."

Statistics compiled by the Canadian Manufacturers' Association also show that women on the job work 30 per cent fewer hours than men.

Sociologist Brigitte Berger of Wellesley College writes: "Both career pattern differences as well as income differences can be explained — and to my mind convincingly — in terms of women's... overall life plans."[33]

American author Janet Radcliffe Richards, in her popular book, *The Skeptical Feminist*, states:

> It is still unfair that individual men (and probably some women too) should have to make large sacrifices.... What about employers who are made to employ women who will do the work less well than men would have done, like the ones at present who are not allowed to take public suspicion of women into consideration? They will lose a great deal of their profit, and therefore are effectively being forced to put some of their effort into improving the position of women, and only some into doing what they themselves want to do. This is the sort of thing Robert Nozick, in his book, *Anarchy, State and Utopia*, would count as forced labor. And what about individual men, who are asked to sacrifice so large a thing as their careers...?

"If justice does not matter in transitions, it does not matter at all," she concluded.[34]

THE LAWS AND ENFORCEMENT

Striking a chill into the hearts and minds of many men and women across the land are the feminist dictators' directives on the enforcement of affirmative action and Equal Pay for Work of Equal Value legislation. Flora MacDonald has promised unlimited resources to the Canadian Human Rights Commission for "policing" (the word most commonly used, as in Iron Curtain countries) all regulations. As federal Minister of Employment and Immigration, she is closely following the recommendations in Judge Rosalie Abella's one-woman report.

However, Flora MacDonald's waffling in regard to the enforcement mechanics for sanctions and penalties is not to be tolerated, according to the feminists. The Minister has argued that the laws would prove self-enforcing, in that those immediately affected, the Crown corporations and federally regulated companies, are required by law to report annually on the facts and figures of their progress.

Mary Cornish, speaking for the Equal Pay Coalition in Ontario, insists that the private sector must also be quickly herded under the same laws, although it has been shown that firms with fewer than fifty employees, which employ half of all female workers, will be severely disadvantaged. While the government is prepared to pay the estimated cost of $90 million annually (one study estimates the cost at $3 billion),[35] such firms in the private sector might face unbearable economic pressures and bankruptcy.

A clause in the 1984 Canada Oil and Gas Act that allows the Energy Minister to require "any company entering into an exploration agreement with the federal government to comply with special Affirmative Action measures as part of the agreement before any work could begin" may simply doom one project after another.

Nevertheless, in Ontario, Attorney-General Ian Scott promised that legislation for Equal Pay for Work of Equal Value would be in place by the fall of 1986 for the province's 68,000 employees. He also promised the introduction of a bill to bring the private sector under such legislation by the end of the year.

"If the government is serious, it will be one of the most dramatic moves ever in the labour field...a level of intervention that has not been seen," Morley Gunderson has pointed out. In the United States, only six state governments have Equal Value legislation, and only for the public sector. Although Britain and some other European countries include the private sector in random policies, there are no records of strict enforcement of the laws.

While Flora MacDonald has hesitated to consider police tactics in terms of penalties and sanctions for enforcement of the federal equality laws, Ontario legislators have assured feminists that their interests will be guaranteed with a $1 million fund provided to support court cases on their behalf. Millions of dollars have actually been pouring into support mechanisms across the country, from federal and provincial governments, to enable women to win all their complaints cases, whereas there has never been a penny offered by governments for defence in these cases.

"The law itself is becoming feminized," according to Eddie Greenspan, one of Canada's best-known criminal lawyers. He told a convention of psychiatrists that "Canadian judges are being intimidated by feminists," and he warned them that

> within ten years the courts will have embraced the entire women's perspective.... Make no mistake about it, this viewpoint is beginning to carry the day in the courtrooms of the land.[36]

Already male judges are facing extreme consequences for expressing opinions during pornography or sexual-assault cases, with feminist groups quick to register formal complaints to judicial councils.

Women are also becoming judges in ever-increasing numbers, and many other lawyers have voiced the fear that it might be humanly impossible for all the future feminist judges to leave their beliefs and bias back at the breakfast table.

Older women judges of exceptional talents, revered in the judicial systems throughout Canada long before the impact of the Women's Liberation Movement, such as Madam Justice Bertha Wilson, of the Supreme Court of Canada; Mary Carter, 61, Judge of the Court of Queen's Bench and the Unified Family Court, Saskatoon; Claire L'Heureux-Dube, 57, Judge of the Quebec Court of Appeal, Quebec City; Constance Glube, 53, Chief Justice of the Trial Division of the Supreme Court of Nova Scotia, naturally welcome the influx of women to all the "courts of justice" in the land. However, even they must question the affirmative action legislation that leapfrogs younger women lawyers past men of much greater seniority, qualifications, and experience, leap-frogging that may be approved and practised throughout the country under the leadership of the federal Minister of Justice, John Crosbie.

The Justice Minister told a meeting of the Canadian Bar Association in St. John's, Newfoundland, in February 1986, that a priority of the Conservative Government was to appoint more women to the bench, and since coming to office he could report a 22 per cent increase in the number of appointments of women judges.

He rejected the recommendations of two Bar Association presentations that judges should not be appointed until their late 40s to ensure their maturity and experience, although, he admitted that "between 45 and 55 was a good age." Notwithstanding, "such an age restriction is arbitrary and would hamstring efforts to get more women on the bench," he said. "We want to increase the number of women on the bench in Canada and there isn't any way we can do it without appointing younger women, because there simply aren't a sufficient number of women lawyers who have been in practice that long."[37]

The Ontario Liberal Government's appointment of Doris Anderson, former president of the Canadian Advisory Council on the Status of Women and later President of the National Action Committee on the Status of Women, to the Ontario Judicial Council, has been seen as a positive step in carrying out federal directives. The Council, a powerful arm of the provincial judiciary, mainly made up of chief justices, considers all proposed appointments of provincial court judges, with its choices accepted by the Attorney-General. Its other duties include investigating complaints against provincial court judges and masters of the Supreme Court of Ontario. A former editor of *Chatelaine*, Ms. Anderson in this judicial position of authority is expected to provide a commanding voice.

7
Society in Limbo and Personal Pain in Transition

There are very few men or women in Canada today who have any clear view of the future — their country's or their own — nor can they fit themselves comfortably into any specific "role."

Only the feminists (growing "more radical with age," the psychologists warn us) would seem to have a comprehensive picture of the coming years and our new society. They apparently see the sexes equal and androgynous, with babies still being produced (sometimes by artificial insemination as in a stud culture, promoted by lesbians), but always the responsibility of the government, with universal child care according to Marxist edicts. In fact, feminist dictators may be able to ensure more and more Marxist control in all areas of society.

However, are the majority of Canadians, men and women, really satisfied with that prognosis?

Wayne Gretzky, our most famous hockey player, has proven: "To win, one must skate to where the puck is going to be — rather than where the puck has been." I believe this advice could be the key to our future.

Of course, history is the greatest teacher of all, followed by the sociology of the present, and both must allow us to look ahead to "where the puck is going to be." Once enlightened, we may be able eventually to exert our democratic rights, to brake, and re-establish balance. We might work on a new set of rules and guidelines, in efforts to lessen the injustices, and ease some of the anguish and confusion in transition.

Our songs, books, and plays are mirroring our anguish and confusion in this transitional period of history.

Listening to the radio as we drove across Canada, we found the airwaves full of bewilderment, questioning, and mourning, in such songs as:

There just isn't any magic here any more...

Whatever happened to old-fashioned love, that would last through the years, through your smiles, through your tears...

My old flame...I can't even think of his name...
My lovers all now seem the same...

Only the lonely know the heartbreak I've been through...

I can't get used to losing you...

I heard the raindrops call your name...

Are you lonely tonight...

Big girls don't cry...

Goodbye, you second-hand man...

Can you tell me where he's gone...

If you go away, if you must, there'll be nothing in the world to trust...

Don't cry out loud... Keep it inside...

Time for you to go...

As soon as I find my shoes, I'm gone...

Know when to walk away, and know when to run...

Don't run out on me...

You won't matter any more...

Annie's taking care of number one...

Lonely woman...

People say that we have always been singing "the blues," but have "the blues" ever before taken over our lives? There were a few words of hope and comfort in Anne Murray's singing of "I Will Survive," and exultation in "I Made it through the Rain," and there was one jubilant song: "Dance, Little Jean. Your Mom is Marrying Your Dad."

Our most famous author, Margaret Atwood, faithfully chronicles the miserable, shabby lives of women, men, and children involved in relationships in her *Life Before Man*.[1] With savage humour and the greatest skill, against a fascinating backdrop of one woman's scientific work with dinosaurs at the Royal Ontario Museum, and the constant overhanging shadow of a failed relationship that led to suicide, the novel grinds inexorably forward, with no answers and no conclusion.

Cross-continental studies in the United States have shown that relationships last, on average, fourteen to twenty months. While formerly they often resulted in

mental anguish, lately they are often simply scored
as satisfactory or less satisfactory interludes. Without
children, women and men may go on and on, seeking
greater satisfaction in each transient attachment, until
they are old or tired or disillusioned and have lost their
confidence in the game of sex.

Plots in Canadian and American fiction are now invariably concerned with transient attachments, the more
dramatic dealing in tragedies. However, there is also a
trend to examine the upbeat ramifications of the Women's
Liberation Movement in the male-female reversal of
roles, as portrayed in The Kitchen Man, by Ira Wood.[2]

The dustjacket advises that the novel depicts a feminist
male, Gabriel, who is first a waiter, then an aspiring
playwright, a babysitter for a lesbian mother, and finally
a stay-at-home, vacuuming, nurturing house companion
for Cynthia, a superwoman divorcee with a teen-age
son. This relationship turns out to be a great success
when Gabriel comes to realize that he has fully accepted,
and in fact enjoys, the reversal in roles.

As the lesbians increase in power in the Canadian
Women's Liberation Movement, more and more books
exploring and commending homosexuality are appearing
on the shelves of Canadian bookstores. Jane Rule's A Hot-
Eyed Moderate,[3] a collection of forty-seven essays that
have been featured in such newspapers and journals as
the now-defunct The Body Politic, and Canadian Literature,
but are not considered moderate, has received rave
reviews.

An American, Jane Rule moved to the Canadian west
coast, which she has found "remarkably rich and nour-
ishing," in 1956. Since then she has lived with a woman
companion, and promoted homosexuality on both sides
of the border in prolific writing in the same vein as Kate
Millett. Her first novel, The Desert of the Heart, dealt
with lesbian love between two women and was made into
a successful movie.[4]

Exploring the homosexual experience, of course, has become the theme of several plays and movies. However, Salem Alaton, reviewing *Hustling* (by writer-director Sky Gilbert, appearing at Toronto's Annex Theatre), in *The Globe and Mail*, saw deeper psychological meanings — "everything but sex" — in the dialogue between three male prostitutes and their clients. He writes:

> Through Alec, Gilbert articulates the best effort of *Hustling*: to take the mask of sexual yearning off the deeper-seated need for affection and understanding that all these men, in their curiously separate ways, are trying to express. In the process, each of the homosexual configurations offered becomes strongly familiar, even indistinguishable from the heterosexual dynamic.

Does this suggest that until the biologists prove that homosexuality is strictly hormonal, we are seeing a great grey area in society, where men come together with men, and women with women, more for reasons of assuaging loneliness than to engage in homosexual acts? Of course, there are still many countries throughout the world that designate homosexuality as an aberration, including the Soviet Union, where homosexual practice is a criminal offence.

The plays and movies of the day also continue to interpret and teach all feminist doctrines, sometimes clumsily. What *The Real Thing* (at The Royal Alexandra Theatre, March 1986) was, Tom Stoppard, a favourite playwright, failed to explain. Was it wife-swapping?

The Clan of the Cave Bear, a movie based on a novel by Jean M. Auel, was filmed in British Columbia by Warner Brothers, and attracts movie-goers in Canada for its spectacular scenery. The ridiculous story — in line with feminist theory — details the adventures of Ayla, separated from her own clan as a child, who is raised by the Cave

Bear Clan of Neanderthals, where she grows up to defy the Neanderthals' traditions by assuming formerly male roles. She becomes the liberated female of her times.

Of course, it was Montreal director Denys Arcand's award-winning production, "The Decline of the American Empire," that celebrated the "liberation" of our times. Men and their wives and girlfriends at a weekend house-party, where the men do the cooking and the women go off to work out at a health club, entertain one another with tales of their sexual exploits, at first in their separate groups, and then at dinner, when confessions are suddenly out of control. There is a sardonic author, who admits her taste for masochism in her love-life; a homosexual professor exulting in his anonymous one-night encounters; and a philandering husband who has revelled in his assortment of sexual adventures, finally exposed to a trusting wife. Cynicism settles as one character suggests: "Our society's frenetic desire for individual happiness may well be linked to the decline of the American Empire."

At the last, friendships and lives are in ruins, and we leave the theatre deeply depressed at this frightening commentary on North American society.

THE ALIENATION OF THE SEXES

In all areas of society, it is apparent that the success of the Women's Liberation Movement in Canada has resulted in the alienation of the sexes. The majority of women seem to have espoused feminist principles, turning their backs on traditional values and attitudes in their "consciousness-raising" and their search for self-fulfillment. At the same time, psychologists now claim that the male response is becoming well defined.

At first bewildered, wounded, and resisting, then angry, sometimes violent, men presently seem to be finally beaten, and resigned to accepting all matriarchal principles. Meanwhile they attempt to match female liberation, self-seeking, and hedonism, with their own determined narcissism.

The most profound changes have occurred in the dispositions, attitudes, aspirations, actually in the very natures, of women and men in Canada during the feminist revolution. Altering their very natures must surely be a matter of the greatest consequence.

Jung, in *The Undiscovered Self*, warned of the consequences. He wrote of

> the question of how the primordial images that maintain the flow of instinctive energy are to be reoriented or readapted. They cannot simply be replaced by a new rational configuration, for this would be molded too much by the outer situation and not enough by man's biological needs. Moreover, not only would it build no bridge to the original man, but it would block the approach to him altogether. This is in keeping with the aims of Marxist education, which seeks, like God himself, to mold man, but in the image of the State.[5]

No longer must a man seek to be strong, protective, chivalrous, and worshipful of the mother-nurturing sex, as women have become stronger than he is, independent, and dedicated to self-sufficiency, self-interest, and self-fulfillment.

Reinventing Womanhood is the title of a feminist book by Carolyn G. Heilbrun, who also wrote *Toward a Recognition of Androgyny*. Both books are important reading in Women's Studies courses.[6]

Psychiatrists see the "altered" nature of women particularly in their alarming rise in crime rates. Throughout the United States and Canada, violent crime among women increases annually. According to statistics released by the Ontario Provincial Secretary of Justice in 1984, the number of women charged in Ontario with Criminal Code offences between 1977 and 1982 (excluding driving infractions) increased 10 per cent, but included a 35 per cent increase in the violent categories, such as assault, robbery and murder. There were 1,832 women so charged in 1978 and 2,480 in 1982.[7] The female bandit, who with her accomplice robbed twenty-one gas stations in nine and a half weeks, gained headlines in *The Toronto Sun*, March 21, 1986.

Alcoholism among women has increased significantly throughout all levels of society.

Our society is no longer surprised at modern women's taking the initiative in all sexual encounters, from dating through courtship to proposals of marriage, although this traditional sequence of events is more often bypassed. Modern women may invite their male acquaintances into their beds even on a first date, and into a relationship soon afterwards. Surveys indicate that women are becoming predators — noticeably in the workplace from the executive positions.

It was William Congreve who spoke the truth when he said, "Hell hath no fury like that of a woman scorned," and in the workplace today it may not be an uncommon occurrence for a female executive to stand in the way of a male employee who has turned his back on her advances. (A young relative of mine certainly suffered such an experience.)

Liberated married men, and older and wiser single men are known to "play along," while the younger single men, at first disillusioned, are soon hardened and grow adept at distancing themselves. The stories of male employers demanding favours from female employees, are now being matched by stories of the reverse, and yet the male complaints are rarely aired publicly, perhaps signifying the last vestiges of chivalry. (Of course, it is common knowledge that a male worker today dare not jostle or even brush against a female worker for fear of being taken to court for sexual harassment — which has certainly widened the gulf between the sexes and heralded the end of office or factory romances).

The "altered" nature of men is seen in the staggering acceleration of male violence against women. "In part, it is a reaction to the new role women are playing in society,"[8] Kathleen Barry, a sociologist at Brandeis University in Waltham, Massachusetts, believes, after completing a 20-year study of the increases in violence and perversions in prostitution. Feminists declare it is the "brute" reaction in men who refuse to accept new feminist-decreed roles in society.

Civilized men seem to be simply walking away, attempting to extricate themselves from their anxieties, uncertainties, and frustrations in their new roles.

Sigmund Freud wrote in his *Civilization and its Discontents*: "Against the suffering which may come upon one from human relationships the readiest safeguard is voluntary isolation, keeping oneself aloof from other people."

Lionel Tiger, in an article in *Chatelaine*, April 1986, discussing the fact that "women now better control their own fertility, and can through various medical advances arrange to have babies without the ongoing participation of men," asked: "Are men redundant?" He claimed:

It's possible they feel not only insecure but redundant. We know that, when people feel powerless, they can become alienated and passive. In this respect, I believe that men as a group have become less responsive to women as a group; that with diminished control they plead diminished responsibility; and that they have difficulty interacting with potential mates in emotionally rich ways.

DIVORCE

Unless a significant proportion of Canadian women decide to fall out of the feminist mainstream, rescuing at least some of the old traditional values and institutions, along with religious principles and a belief in monogamy, the pundits across the country who are predicting, not higher divorce rates, but simply the end of the institution of marriage, will be proven accurate in their forecasts.

Statistics across the continent show the enormous percentage of marriages that are now dissolved within the first three years. It is truly inconceivable how many of these marriages last three weeks in the present climate of self-seeking.

Marriages of the past endured with unselfishness on the part of one mate one week, and unselfishness on the part of the other mate the next week. Marriages were built on sensitivity, understanding, communications, and giving, giving, giving — overcoming large and small differences and difficulties one week, and finding large and small joys the following week. Sometimes, the give-and-take could be a lop-sided exchange, one way or the other, and often there was subtle (as opposed to raucous) readjustment. However, when the exchange was fairly even, a marriage could root and grow, strong enough to endure life's storms, and creative enough to contribute warmth and service to neighbourhoods or even world communities.

Such marriages indeed touched those inside and outside the family dwelling. The wife could be a housewife or a doctor, or work with her husband in the store or on the farm, reasonably happy in her particular choice of lifestyle. In attitude, she was always *naturally stereotyped as unselfish*.

The modern feminist attitude to marriage was effectively demonstrated at the Royal Alexandra Theatre in Toronto during a production of the old-fashioned musical, *The Boy Friend*. The heroine, in love and dreaming of her own little love nest and her dear husband coming home tired from work, dances across the stage with his slippers. A hoot of derision was heard from every corner of the theatre, performance after performance. (I checked with the ushers.)

Would anyone believe that there is still a woman who will fetch her husband's slippers when he comes home and flops into a chair after heaving hundred-pound cases on and off a truck all day? Such an overt expression of "caring," the feminists have told us, is simply unacceptable servitude acknowledging "oppression." And we have been fed such wicked caricatures of undeserving "macho" men — for example, Archie Bunker, and Celie's loathsome husband in *The Color Purple*.

Government funds are helping to destroy that former "unselfish" female stereotype, by introducing and promoting the new replacement stereotypes. A National Film board release, *Growing up Female*, "has become a classic statement on oppressive conditioning and socialization of girls and women" which is no longer acceptable. The promotion for *In The Best Interests of Children* reads: "This forceful film about the issue of child custody for lesbian mothers is a loving portrait of women and children and will *destroy* many stereotypes."[9]

According to Statistics Canada, the divorce rate rose 82 per cent between 1973 and 1983, but had risen 500 per cent since 1968. In 1973 there were indications that 97 per cent of males and 93 per cent of females would marry at least once in their lifetime, but in 1983, the projected percentages dropped to 65 per cent. At the same time, extensive surveys are indicating that few women over the age of 30 will have any opportunity to marry, as more and more men find less and less incentive in the connubial picture.

It was Ann Landers who dispelled the notion that modern marriage even promised a satisfying sex life for either partner. When 90,000 respondents to an informal poll informed her that they preferred "cuddling" to intercourse, psychiatrists across the country were quick to point out that satisfying sex depends on time and energy, and that working mothers would have little of either at the end of their two-career days.[10] Dr. Katrina Eastwood, a Toronto physician and sex therapist, claims, "It is not uncommon for some couples to go for a month or more without making love."[11]

If happy gatherings around a dining-room table, with family members sharing the experiences of the day, were a former incentive toward marriage and family life, that may also be a tradition of the past. Mary Powers, a director of the Good Housekeeping Institute, describes modern eating habits, particuarly among the professional classes, as a "non-meal phenomenon," without scheduled mealtimes, and with all members of the family "grazing" on a snack here and a snack there, often in front of the television. In Canada, today, couples are spending their two-career salaries on restaurant eating as well, with 11 per cent of Canada's $17.9 billion restaurant business now going to a rising breakfast market.[12]

The CBC's Sunday Morning Food Show reported that North Americans who do cook average thirty minutes a day preparing meals, while British housewives spend at least an hour, and the French homemaker may lovingly devote three hours a day to the creation of family meals.

Articles in American publications are also regretting the demise of cleanliness and order and the time for gardening in modern living. According to Selling Areas Marketing, a 20-year-old Time Inc. division that measures supermarket sales, there has been a steady decline in sales of all heavy-duty cleaning items during the past five years. A woman's life now is centred in the workplace. Carolyn Forte, director of Good Housekeeping's Home Care Department, believes: "There's a whole new generation of women who wouldn't be caught dead on their hands and knees scrubbing a floor."[13]

Few men contemplating marriage in a feminist world will look forward to being "broken in" to all household tasks, particularly if they labour physically throughout the day. Of course, sons from traditional homes, where the word "evening" itself denoted peace or fun, and always relaxation, may never be ready to accept their new roles.

Still, marriage as an institution must endure, according to a national survey — even in its unattractive, divorce-ridden, less-than-satisfactory form. Canadians are definitely not willing to adopt an alternative such as that set forth in *The Dialectic of Sex* by Shulamith Firestone, one of the many influential feminist writers in the United States. Arguing that marriage could not fulfill the needs of men and women because it was "organized around and reinforces a fundamentally oppressive biological condition," she suggested that "our concept of exclusive physical partnerships" must disappear from our "psychic structure," that children be born to a unit, and that the blood tie of the mother to the child be eventually severed.[14]

The Dialectic of Sex is no longer compulsory reading in Women's Studies courses throughout the United States, although it continues to be avidly read by students in the hundreds of Women's Studies programs which multiply year after year in our own Canadian universities.

There are concerted efforts to revive and restore marriage and its traditional values throughout the United States, with a groundswell emanating out of Washington. At the same time, psychologists and sociologists feverishly seek answers to the 50 per cent American divorce rate. Some of their studies indicate that in a feminist world where both partners are conditioned to absolute independence, there is always a view of greener pastures ahead, toward other marriages, which in the majority of cases do not materialize. The younger couples, particularly, seem to rush into divorce, lacking the patience or foresight to struggle through the large and small problems, to capture the large and small joys.

Instead, in divorce, always if there are children, they will find the large and small agonies. One woman wrote: "There were 50 problems in our marriage — but there are 500 in our divorce."

When two people reach an insurmountable impasse, divorce may be the only answer, but even then the after-effects may prove devastating. There could be extreme grieving on the part of either or both spouses, involving rejection, humiliation or guilt. If it deepens, this often develops into hysteria, depression, and sometimes a paralysis of will, until there is acceptance and resignation, according to psychiatrists.

The economic disadvantages of divorced mothers are dealt with in hundreds of articles in Canadian publications. Their lifestyles deteriorate significantly, with an estimated 75 per cent of former husbands and fathers defaulting on support payments. To remedy this situation in the United States, President Reagan signed a bill allowing all state governments to garnishee a defaulter's wages, while in Canada Parliament proceeds with similar legislation.

It has been costing Canadian taxpayers $1 billion a year to support dependent spouses and their children through social service programs, federal Justice Minister John Crosbie told the Ontario Bar Association. He promised that the new laws would facilitate tracing defaulters, and allow federal income tax refunds to be garnisheed for payments.[15]

Manitoba already has effective legislation, with each court order registered in a Winnipeg computer. As soon as a payment is missed, the computer prints out an alert for an enforcement officer, with power to garnishee wages. In Alberta and British Columbia determined defaulters are going to jail in escalating numbers.[16]

Senior Justice L.A. Beaulieu of Metro Toronto, Peel

and York regions, has pointed out that the violation of support payments is the only civil court matter for which a jail term can be meted out as a penalty.

(One hopes Canadians will never see anything as drastic as the pre-dawn "support raids" carried out by sheriff's deputies in Marlboro, Maryland, a Washington suburb, when eighty men were swept out of their homes and jailed for non-payment.)[17]

The injustice perpetrated by the courts in automatically awarding sole custody of the children to the mother in 85.6 per cent of all Canadian divorces involving dependent children — whether the mother works outside the home or not — is never noted, except by Statistics Canada (1983). *Statistics also show that women outnumber men two to one in seeking divorce.*

Disadvantaged fathers have become bitter and vengeful when they have been denied or impeded in visiting rights, and have often moved from their home provinces to get away from the pain, while they attempt to punish the wife with nonpayment of alimony and child support. One father, blocked for three years from seeing or even talking to two adored children (he was dutifully paying all costs), packed a small bag with everything he claimed he had left from a good job and an eight-year marriage, and flew to Australia. He belonged to a Fathers' Rights group that had lobbied in Ottawa, unsuccessfully, to have joint-custody provisions included in Canada's 1986 Divorce Act.

We see hundreds of other fathers, sometimes awkwardly playing with small children in the parks — fathers and very small children may become strangers in two-week lapses — while McDonald's reports a constant flow of fathers and their children at all meals throughout their access weekends.

One such father has described his special, sometimes unbearable agony in picking up his three children every other weekend at his former home, where his former wife is now engaged in a "relationship," with her lover enjoying his children, his home, even all the furniture he helped choose and paid for, as well as the garden he had so lovingly planted (the garden has become very important in his mind as he grieves in a barren bachelor apartment). This friend admitted jokingly, we hope jokingly, that he has considered suicide — or murder.

SINGLE MOTHERS

Meanwhile, the growing number of single mothers is reaching epidemic proportions, with a large percentage of them bcoming welfare recipients at staggering costs to all governments.

Granted, there are single mothers, true feminists, who have chosen sole parenthood and have the determination and means to attempt to make this a successful and satisfying lifestyle.

But then there are the thousands of young single mothers who have simply found themselves the victims of a feminist society, that has established, as the dominant values, self-fulfillment, hedonism, a basic contempt of men, and contempt for former traditional values.

I have a friend who is a typical victim. She was married at 18 to an Air Canada pilot, and had planned a traditional stay-at-home motherhood with a small baby, when she suddenly discovered that her husband was living part time with a stewardess in another city. "How could you object?" he asked. "It is 1972 and we are living in a *liberated* age." Devastated, she took the baby back to her home and parents in a small Ontario city, sued for divorce, and got a good job.

Later, she moved in with a company associate whom she admired extravagantly. He had two boys, she had the one girl, and for three years she was convinced that they were a contented, integrated "family." When she became pregnant again, she was certain that they would marry, only to be shocked beyond belief when he explained: "Sarah, you are the loveliest, finest person I will ever know, but nothing on earth would persuade me to risk marriage a second time."

Sarah let him believe she would have an abortion, but instead returned to have the baby at home with her parents, who then cared for her two children when she was able to go back to work. Both parents have since died, and now she struggles to give her children all the warmth and love she worries that they are missing in a one-parent, no-grandparent household. Fortunately, she has reached an executive position in her firm, so they do not lack monetary benefits. She also suspects her situation is easier in a small city than it would be in a large urban area, as she has considerable neighbourhood support.

Still, she has experienced terrible loneliness and near-serious depression — the loneliness, despair, and depression affecting a large percentage of our population today, men and women who are living their private lives without adult companions.

LONELINESS

The number of men and women living alone in Canada rose from 800,000 in 1971 to 1.7 million in 1981. There are 500,000 living alone in Metro Toronto, according to Statistics Canada, including 24,000 separated men, 34,000 separated women, 21,000 divorced men and 36,000 divorced women. In the United States, the Census figures showed that the number of adults over the age of 18 years living alone, rose from 53.1 million in 1970 to 71.3 million in 1983. In a 1985 report, single-person households totalled 19.9 million, 23 per cent of all American households. [18]

In both countries, resulting loneliness as a major social problem has become the subject of urgent studies by psychiatrists and other mental health experts. The National

Institute of Mental Health in Bethesda, Maryland, estimates that depressive disorders cost the United States $20 billion a year in treatment and lost productivity, and Canadian costs may be comparative to population. At the same time, other researchers are beginning to establish that loneliness is a major component in depression, which in turn causes physical illnesses, with inestimable costs.

The biochemical changes that take place in the body when one is alone, without a companion in whom one may confide, have been noted by a husband-and-wife team at Ohio State University. Extensive tests by microbiologist Ronald Glazer and behavioural psychologist Janice K. Kiecolt-Glazer found that changes in the white blood-cell count caused by loneliness and stress hampered the body's ability to fight disease.[19]

In the authoritative magazine, *Science*, in April 1986, Bernard Dixon reported on studies being carried out at the British Medical Research Council's Common Cold Unit (situated near Salisbury) that have proven "that this relatively trivial infection is affected by the psyche."

Studies seeking further correlation between loneliness, stress, anxieties, ensuing depression, and more serious illnesses such as cancer and heart and circulatory disease are being conducted in many research centres in Europe, Canada, and the United States. The insidious progress from loneliness to mental and physical illness is often seen to begin with headaches, back problems, alcohol, and drugs.

"Loneliness: America's #1 Mental Health Problem," was the title of a major article in *Woman's World*, January 28, 1986, that claimed that one in four Americans was a sufferer. The article quoted the findings of psychologists that indicated clearly that all people *need* two kinds of relationships: intimate relationships, such as with spouses, children, and parents, and social relationships, such as with friends, neighbours, and business acquaintances.

The most poignant commentary on society today is surely the surge in the teddy bear industry, as recorded in staggering 1985 Christmas sales, and in continuing sales — with teddy bears a most popular gift from one adult to another.

Loneliness in Sweden is now being faced by government and health authorities as a social crisis, largely responsible for the country's world-leading suicide rate. In a population of 8.3 million people, 3.7 million live alone, 2 million of them men, 1.7 million of them women. Hotlines enabling desperately lonely people contemplating suicide to talk to a priest are constantly jammed, twenty-four hours a day. In the Stockholm area alone in 1984, there were 95,000 calls from lonely people threatening to take their own lives.[20]   = more alone than married!

SUICIDE

In Canada and the United States, the suicide rates are climbing alarmingly.

One American commits suicide every twenty minutes, according to a report released by the Atlanta Centers for Disease Control, and it warns that suicide has become "a serious public health problem." An astonishing rise in the suicide rate among women has been acknowledged by the American Association of Suicidology, a research body based in Los Angeles, where the rate in the 15-30 age group has increased over 600 per cent since 1963. Twice as many women as men are known to be on tranquillizers and other forms of psychotropic drugs, and two-thirds of the 50,000 people who died of tranquillizer overdoses in 1984 in the United States were women.[21]

In Canada, 73 per cent of all tranquillizer prescriptions are made out for women and girls, and may be providing a means of self-destruction on this side of the border, as well. (Figures are not available.) However, in 1983, there were three times more men than women among the 3,755 Canadians who took their own lives, and this ratio remains constant, with the 20-to-29-year-old group accounting for the greatest number.[22]

A 12-member task force, appointed by the federal government to investigate the increasing incidence and underlying causes of suicide in Canada, has found that young adults and men and women who are divorced or separated are the high-risk groups.

Dr. Syer-Solursh, chairman of the task force, believes that the police, teachers, social workers, physicians, and nurses, to whom lonely, desperate people contemplating suicide may turn, are not trained to "recognize, assess or manage" this volatile situation, and that there must be special courses created in police and teachers' colleges, and in schools of social work and medicine to prepare them.[23]

Meanwhile, the Canadian Association for Suicide Prevention has been established as a national emergency measure.

THE PLAGUE

One might imagine that our troubled society has now been dealt a final blow, with the onset of AIDS and our ensuing uncontrolled panic.

AIDS (acquired immune deficiency syndrome), first identified by Dr. Luc Montagnier at the Pasteur Institute in Paris in 1982, is now designated "the plague of the Eighties," a terrifying and always fatal sexually transmitted disease destroying the immune system that normally protects us. There were 649 cases reported in Canada by November 1986, and based on the recorded rate of the spread of the disease — the figures double every seven and a half months — the number of Canadians who may contract the disease could reach 20,000 by the year 1990.

Dr. Evelyn Wallace, senior medical consultant for the disease control and epidemiology division of the Ontario

Ministry of Health, speaking to a workshop at the Ontario Public Health Association in Toronto, also predicted that AIDS will overtake vehicle accidents and suicide to become the leading killer of men between the ages of 30 and 39 in the province. While AIDS mainly affects the homosexual community (homosexual men have accounted for 93 per cent of the cases recorded in Ontario), it is still considered only a matter of time before an increasing number of heterosexuals are afflicted in crossover contacts.[24]

The trend has been confirmed in the United States, where there were 13,402 cases of AIDS already reported by September 1985. Consequently, Dr. James Curran, chief of AIDS research at the Centers for Disease Control in Atlanta, estimated that between 500,000 and 1 million Americans had already been exposed to the virus, with the projected probability that 10 per cent of them must fall victim to the disease.

Unless general promiscuity throughout the population is somehow halted, many medical researchers predict that one in ten North Americans, including 20 to 30 per cent of college-age women, will eventually become infected through sexual contacts.

In utter panic, the state of Texas has revived an old state law forbidding sodomy, in a desperate effort to help control the alarming spread of AIDS in that state. This action was upheld by the Fifth U.S. Circuit Court of Appeals in New Orleans, with the reminder that all states have the right to legislate on questions of morality. (Russia claims it is free of AIDS because of its enforcement of anti-sodomy laws.)

While scientists across the continent and in Europe feverishly seek medication at least to retard the inexorable progress of the fatal AIDS, other sexually communicable diseases are becoming resistant to formerly highly effective antibiotics. They are no longer responding to any control measures, and are producing the "Number 1 health problem in the world," according to Immunology and Microbiology Professor Richard Morisset, of the University of Montreal. In the United States, newly graduated family doctors have reported that every twentieth person in their new practices is seeking treatment for venereal disease.

The "liberation" in the Women's Liberation Movement that has endorsed promiscuity of both sexes, without any moral restraints, is seen as a major factor in the multiplying of all venereal diseases.

"We are a sick, sick society," thunder the fundamentalist preachers across America — "We are living in a Sodom and Gomorrah."

BIRTH DEARTH

However, it may not be a wall of fire that will finally overtake us but our plunging birth rate. Canada now has one of the lowest fertility rates in the world, 1.4 children per family, half its 1957 level. Traditional families are fast disappearing altogether; the use of contraceptives, including the new, widespread acceptance of vasectomies and female sterilization, mean that Canada's population of 25 million, achieved in November 1983, could sag back to 15 million by 2050, as government population experts have predicted.[25]

In 1974, former federal Liberal Minister of Immigration Otto Lang advised doubling Canada's population through immigration to meet our population crisis.

Scientists studying the alarming slide in American fertility figures at the Office of Population Research at Princeton University have suggested that women may eventually have to be paid to have babies.[26]

Motherhood is certainly no longer a priority of the modern feminist, but is only an option to be freely chosen, if it fits into the individual's ambitions for self-fulfillment. Western women have been well schooled in the Women's Liberation Movement's theory that biology has simply proven a female "trap" since the begining of time. Now vanquished by choice, by contraception and abortions, it must never again be allowed to control a woman's life. *12*

I am always puzzled when a woman in one of the science disciplines proves herself a feminist (such as anthropologist Margaret Mead). Any study of non-human species — birds, animals, underwater creatures — always shows the importance of the biological considerations which the feminists seek to deny.

Surgical sterilization has become the most popular method of contraception for both females and males in the United States, a report from the National Center for Health Statistics in Washington confirms. In Canada, sterilization is also becoming a common alternative for female and male singles, as well as for married couples and those in common-law relationships, according to studies such as that undertaken by Evelyne Lapierre-Adamcyk, a University of Montreal sociologist, who questioned 5,300 Canadian women between the ages of 18 and 49.

Another Quebec study, by Dr. Pierre Assalian, director of the Human Sexuality Program at the Montreal General Hospital, has found that the Women's Liberation Movement has contributed to impotence and a lower sex drive in many men. This complaint of 50 per cent of all patients seeking sexual therapy, he attributes to the modern woman's aggressiveness in and out of bed. Other experts believe there are some thoroughly intimidated men showing up in statistics, who are simply retreating into celibacy, having lost all trust in women.[27]

Their increasing numbers are producing another saddening class of Canadians, the thousands of beautiful young women who are to remain the unwilling "spinsters" of feminist times. Studies across the continent indicate that their probability of meetings and marriages is sinking steadily year after year.

Hundreds of magazine articles now advise young women where they may meet young men — other than at the bars, which have proven good only for one-night stands. The workplace is most often recommended, but men have become wary of making overtures in the workplace, because of the unclear laws covering harassment. At the same time, churches and synagogues, traditionally ideal meeting places, again seek to attract young single adults.

QUEBEC'S JEOPARDY

by PQ nationalist / Socialist

It may be one of the greatest tragedies in Canadian history if René Levesque's historic efforts to save the French culture and language on this continent is finally defeated by the Women's Liberation Movement. In Quebec, as across Canada, women have been liberated from traditional morality, the traditional home, and more crucially in Quebec, from their traditional Church. If they are happier, that has yet to be recorded, but the Quebec fertility rate has been recorded. From one of the highest fertility rates in the western world prior to the Sixties, Quebec has moved to one of the lowest rates, declining 62 per cent.

"There is not an area in the world that has had such a spectacular drop," stated Georges Mathews, a demographer at the Institut Nationale de la Récherche Scientifique, and a consultant to a National Assembly Committee, which was appointed to study what has come to be considered a provincial problem of the greatest urgency. He has recommended a substantial increase in the family allowance for the third child, as one measure to reverse the continuing trend. Other experts advise new immigration policies, allowing in waves of French-speaking immigrants from France and other francophone countries such as those in Africa.[28]

The feminist influence in the arts in Quebec is seen as the major factor in changing the Quebec woman, formerly a veritable stereotype of the ideal traditional wife and mother, with her interests centred in the home, into the married or single career woman, like her English-speaking counterpart, with her life and main interests now centred in the workplace. There has been very powerful persuasion in such novels as Marie-Claire Blais' feminist novel, *Les Nuits de L'Underground*; in popular drama, such as Denise Boucher's feminist play, *Les Fées Ont Soif*; and in the poetry of many feminist poets, such as that of Nicole Brossard.

Few French-Canadian daughters now enter the old religious orders, famous throughout the world for their ministries to the poor, as the provincial government is now expected to provide the agencies for all social aid services. The little nuns, in their grey and black habits, whose very appearance often spelled comfort, hope, and succor, are now seldom seen on the streets of Montreal.

In the United States, even some of the most "liberated" feminists have come to recognize approaching disaster, in the final annihilation of a former culture, unless there is a halt, and sometimes a reversal of feminist direction.

Margaret Mead, in her later articles in *Redbook*, the magazine to which she contributed for seventeen years, was suddenly admonishing American women to adopt new guidelines. She wrote: "Can we restore family stability... can we move to a firm belief that living in a family is worth a great effort...? We shall have to accept willingly the cost of what must be done, realizing that whatever we do ultimately will be less costly than our present sorry attempts to cope with breakdown and disaster...."[29]

8
The Children

Children may be the greatest sufferers and the greatest
losers in our transitional society, for they are not yet the
absolute responsibility of legislatures, federal and provincial, as they would be in the communist countries.

In addition to all the remarkably talented backbone
Canadians who will never be born to all the talented
young women and men in Canada, because they are not
marrying or they are not having children, there are the
children who, having been born, are presently existing
under serious handicaps: the little people of the poor,
the middle class, and the wealthy, in wretchedly inadequate daytime "orphanages"; the children hanging on to
their mothers' jeans in the food bank line-ups (at least
half of those mothers are truly not responsible for their
miserable plight, but simply victims of a society that has
persuaded them to divorce, to hate men, and that it is
normal and acceptable to rear children without fathers);
the children born into lesbian households; the children
who were conceived and born for the further self-

124

fulfillment of single mothers, or perhaps simply to assuage adult loneliness, also denied fathers; the millions of children, who are the permanently wounded and grieving casualties of the divorce battlegrounds; the many teen-agers in our rootless society, drowning in alcohol, drugs, and sex; the teen-agers, and younger children, as well, who have turned to lives of crime, from petty crime to murder; the teen-age runaways from impossible home situations, which in most cases, according to statistics, involve stepparents. A significant proportion of the latter are now the teen-age prostitutes, living and dying on the streets of our big cities, or the teen-agers in utter despair who are commiting suicide in ever-increasing numbers.

Do we not care that our present and future generations of children may be doomed? Are hedonism and self-fulfillment really more important than the life and times of our children? Are all the strong and nurturing links between generations, forged in the old traditional families, to be permanently severed?

Finally, is there any way we can address the problems facing our children of all ages, short of asking hundreds of thousands of mothers (not the sole-support mothers, whom we must never forsake, or the wondermothers who are able to divide their minds and bodies and spirits into two parts, one for the workplace and one for the fireside), to return home to care for their own children, restoring some stability, security, and even morality to their lives, and to society as a whole.

Such mothers may be encouraged to learn the skills of creative, patient, and rewarding motherhood, instead of motherhood-on-the-run. Perhaps the Canadian public could also be re-educated to believe again that motherhood and homemaking are as noble a profession as any other, and in fact, may offer a woman more rewards than any other.

DAY CARE

The child care situation throughout Canada was in crisis by 1986. This was spelled out in no uncertain terms in a 400-page report, costing $900,000. Compiled by a ministerial task force appointed by the former federal Liberal government two years earlier, it recognized the urgency of the accompanying problems.

Shocking facts came out in the hearings that were held in five Canadian cities, with 200 organizations and groups presenting briefs, in addition to the 7,000 written submissions from parents. "The vast majority of Canadian children, more than 80 per cent, are in the care of unlicensed care-givers... the major disadvantage of unlicensed care is that it is not subject to even minimal standards; there is no system of quality control upon which parents can rely,"[1] it concluded.

The task force, headed by Dr. Katie Cooke, a British Columbia sociologist, included other eminent experts in the field: Ruth Rose-Lizée, former economics professor at the University of Quebec in Montreal; Jack London, a Manitoba law professor; and Renée Edwards, former executive director of the Victoria Day Care Services in Toronto. They recommended a gradual increase in the supply of publicly-funded day care extending to the year 2001, when a universal system could be in place (as in Russia), with a "total annual cost of $11.3 billion."

Michael Krashinsky, an economist at the University of Toronto, claims that the figure would be closer to $40 billion a year, if salaries in the system rose toward those in the public-school system.[2] However, in addition, the report suggested that our economy would also have to support more time off for parents to care for children, with expanded unemployment benefits for those parents.

Our poor children, when reaching adulthood, will then have to pay for their own childhood day care — in our ensuing government deficits. Leading economists *then why consult?*

across Canada emphasize that any such increasing program, even leading to the lower estimated figure of $11.3 billion annually, would put an impossible drain on public resources unless we are prepared to organize and allot our resources as in a communist state. The Women's Liberation Movement may have been moving us in this general direction.

In the federal study, most Canadians agreed that child care for the children of single mothers must be considered a government priority, but the task force admitted that there was strong opposition to a universal approach that could result in all children's being enrolled in the system.

However, feminist lobby groups across the country refusing to countenance opposition to universality, which is one of their principal platforms, forced the federal Conservative government to undertake another $1 million survey of the situation, sending eight members of Parliament across the country in a repetitive exercise.[3]

On March 7, 1987, *The Toronto Star* reported that Jake Epp, federal Minister of Health, was still questioning public response. "When you ask 'should the government pay totally when a family has two parents in the paid labour force?'... the polls indicate that less than 10 per cent support that option," he said.

Meanwhile, more than a million and a half of our children appear to be in serious danger, with their physical, mental, and spiritual needs, for most of their waking hours, in the hands of basically untrained, unskilled, and often unloving keepers.

Even licensed day care centres have been found to be chronically understaffed, and serving inadequate food, with questionable sanitary facilities that could and do lead to the spread of illnesses. Inspection is often inadequate as well, as in Metro Toronto, where there are only nine Ontario government inspectors covering 605 licensed day care centres.

The most alarming trend in Canada, according to many pediatric specialists, is in the numbers of mothers now leaving children under the age of three in such care, as pediatric studies indicate that the first three years of life are critical in all areas of a child's development.[4] More than 50 per cent of Canadian women in two-parent families work outside the home, and by 1984, 52 per cent of mothers with children under the age of three were in the labour force. This number is steadily increasing (there was a 62 per cent increase between 1976 and 1984).

It was Dr. Elliott Barker, a forensic psychiatrist at Ontario's maximum-security facility at Penetanguishene, who termed day care centres for children under three "part-time orphanages." Children in such centres are unable to form "close, stable bonds" with constantly changing and rotating caretakers, and consequently fail to develop the qualities of "trust, empathy and affec-tion," he believes. He warned that "in 15 years we could be faced with a generation of psychopaths — adults who are superficial, manipulative and unable to maintain lasting, mutually satisfactory relationships with others."[5]

In the United States there have been hundreds of day care abuse cases before the courts, resulting in the insurance rates for day care centres rising between 300 and 600 per cent. American parents are consistently advised against placing their children in centres without insurance, as even the legendary minor falls may have serious after-effects. Children who become suddenly ill in day care centres may always be at great risk. While "Sniffles Retreats" for day care charges have become a part of the day care scene in the United States, no such facilities seem to be available in Canada.

CHILDREN OF DIVORCE

The Women's Liberation Movement only reached a

crescendo in the Seventies, with the acceleration of discontented women turning against men generally, and leaving their homes in steadily increasing numbers. In Canada one in every three marriages, and in the United States one in every two ends in separation or divorce. The devastating effect on the children of divorce has yet to be conclusively assessed.

However, the children of divorce (as well as other children in single-parent situations), are being proven the greatest losers in all current studies. They may become poor students — 40 per cent of them are low achievers; they are definitely sick more often; they are absent from school more often; are more likely to play truant than other students, and twice as likely to drop out of school before graduating; finally, they are apt to face unemployment, with many of them unemployable; and many will procreate another generation like themselves.[6]

When your parents get divorced, you cry every night...and you want the terrible trouble to go away, but it doesn't...and you blame yourself, you're a wicked child....Then your Mommy tells you it is not your fault, it is your Daddy's...but you don't want it to be Daddy's fault either....It is so mixed up....You cry and cry, but no one wants you to cry...so you only cry at night....[7]

These exact words, with many variations, have been repeated to social researchers thousands of times by distressed children.

Children lose their fathers in divorce in 90 per cent of all cases on the North American continent. It can be no small loss, losing a parent, and has been recorded consistently as a trauma far harder for a child to adapt to than death. Death they will eventually become resigned to, while, unconsciously, they may never accept the divorce of their parents. Pediatric psychiatrists have come to believe that the pain and despair they suffer at the initial breakup may then fester, destroying all hope of a happy, normal adulthood.[8] A significant proportion of them will never marry; they will be unable to form trusting and meaningful relationships; they may have no desire for children of their own; they may explore homo-sexuality as an alternative to heterosexuality; and they may end up old and bitter singles with little to live for.

Dr. Judith Wallerstein, a leading American expert in social work and law, and head of the "Center for the Family in Transition," in Corte Madera, California, found considerable evidence in a ten-year study of sixty families and 131 children, aged two to 18, that divorce can place "a prolonged mental, physical and emotional burden on children."[9]

She points out that in many divorced families, a custodial parent's "child-rearing capacities" deteriorated. She has also listed the four groups of children she has found the most divorce-troubled: those forced to take inordinate responsibility for their own upbringing; those who must become the main source of emotional support for parent or siblings; those who remain the targets of continuing disputes between parents; and those who experience a second divorce and cannot cope the second time. After five years, she recorded that 37 per cent of the children were suffering from various forms of depression.

Dr. H. Paul Gabriel, professor of clinical psychiatry at the New York University Medical Center, claims that "All children today fear losing a parent... there is nothing about which they worry more."[10]

Furthermore, children are no longer taught to believe in family security. New York University psychology professor Paul C. Vitz, appointed by the American government's National Institute of Education to do a study of American public-school textbooks, found that the traditional family had been reduced to "people you live with." Never anywhere in the texts were the words "marriage," "husband," or "homemaker" used. Women were invariably presented in the workplace, and there was nothing to suggest that "homemaking is an important job."[11]

In his report, Dr. Vitz also regretted "the absence of any concern for non-material values... only money, status and enjoyment being presented as motivations for work, with no indication than many work out of concern for others, or because of the intrinsic value of certain kinds of work." Specific references to religion had been deliberately omitted — even the Pilgrim Fathers' First Thanksgiving, with the Pilgrims simply described as "people who make long trips."

Although comparative studies have not been undertaken in Canada, this also seems to be the general direction of our Canadian educational system in a matriarchy. Of course, feminism, rooted in its search for self-fulfillment and in its hedonistic theories, has always been incompatible with all religious teachings.

How can children emotionally survive the turbulence and lack of security in "serial marriages"? Margaret Mead, who had been married three times, often remarked that she considered three marriages to be the ideal number — one for children, one for sex, and one for companionship.[12] Lynne Gordon's fascinating book, *Working Without a Net: My Intimate Memoirs*, published by McClelland and Stewart in April 1986, was a personal account of her three marriages, and undoubtedly was designed to help other women cope with their problems in transitions.[13]

It is strange to look back and realize how many Canadians may have been shocked in 1970, only seven years after the introduction of the Women's Liberation Movement on this continent, when Alvin Toffler in his classic work, *Future Shock,* predicted "serial marriages."

"Couples will enter matrimony knowing from the start that the relationship is short-lived..." he had written in his chapter dealing with "The Fractured Family."[14]

MISSING CHILDREN

In the United States, it has been established by police records that 95 per cent of kidnapped children have been abducted by their own non-custodial parents (with fathers being apprehended and convicted of the crime in every state in the Union). Most of the missing teen-agers are runaways. The Federal Bureau of Investigation, listing 35,000 children under the age of 18 as missing, reported that there were fewer than 100 active cases nationwide of children known to be taken by strangers.

The exact figures in Canada have been inestimable, due to lack of available information, but growing panic at the increasing incidence of "missing children" has resulted in a national research project dealing with the problem, initiated by Solicitor-General Perrin Beatty. (There were 2,400 children under the age of 16 listed as missing in Metro Toronto in 1985.) At the same time, a Central Registry has been set up by the Royal Canadian Mounted Police in Ottawa, to disseminate information across the country with the co-operation of all provincial and local police forces, in an effort to meet another social crisis of our times.[15]

CHILDREN IN STEPFAMILIES

We know that a majority of children suffer in varying degrees in stepfamilies, even when there is a dramatic economic improvement in their lifestyles.

No less a giant than world-famous Dr. Benjamin Spock has called stepparenthood "a naturally accursed relationship." His own experiences as one by his own admission drove him to a family therapist, and into an intensive study of a common modern dilemma. However, if his book, *Baby and Child Care*, was to solve a multitude of child-rearing problems for generations of mothers, his present advice on stepparenting, in countless articles and television interviews, is considered less helpful. In his own case, time alone proved the principal healer.[16]

Erna Paris, Toronto journalist, in her book, *Stepfamilies: Making Them Work* (Avon, 1984), claims that the difficulties in stepparenthood must never be underestimated, and that only great understanding, patience, and perseverance can bring about peace and a satisfactory truce. Many such studies have shown that miserable, suffering children of all ages are usually responsible for the failure of the one-half of all remarriages that terminate in divorce on this continent.

LATCHKEY CHILDREN AND TEEN-AGE PREGNANCIES

Canadian society, in 1986, suddenly became aware of the dangers that could be encountered by the latchkey children of working mothers, and the serious consequences of their growing numbers. Statistics Canada had reported in 1982 that there were 522,000 children between the ages of six and 14 who had no one to take care of them after school.

In Edmonton, the Committee for the Preservation of Out-of-School Care, made up of concerned parents and child care experts, instituted a study that found that there were 32,000 to 40,000 Edmonton children between the ages of five and 14 years, who had mothers working outside the home. Only one in ten of these children came from a single-parent family. The resulting widely distributed, 20-page report indicated that a lack of after-school adult care was causing Edmonton children to become poor students, "anxious, frustrated and alienated ...some playing hookey, running away from home... and driven toward delinquency, drug abuse, and even suicide."[17]

Jake Kuiken, a Calgary child development consultant, believes that children who are consistently left alone have heightened levels of fear, with fright in the five-to-10-year-olds turning into depression in the teen-agers. Many surveys have proven that those children have a greater number of home accidents. The teen-agers are more apt to smoke and drink, and they may feel intense pressure to grow up too fast.[18]

It is true that many teen-age boys and girls are expected to grow up too fast. Where mothers are working outside the home, they are often burdened with an inordinate amount of housework and family grocery shopping. In recognition of their influence in the supermarkets a New York study was commissioned by advertisers, to take into account the grocery-shopping choices of thousands of teen-agers.[19]

Latchkey children, home alone while their mothers are at work, are also more likely to engage in sex than other children, according to a major study by a husband-and-wife team. Thomas Long, a professor at the Catholic University of America, and Lynette Long, an associate professor at American University in Washington, D.C. (the latter, a former principal of an elementary school who first noticed the amazing numbers of children wearing house-keys on strings around their necks, coined the expression "latchkey children"), interviewed 400 children between the ages of 12 and 15 across the United States. They found that "teenagers these days don't get pregnant in motels and cars at 10 o'clock at night....Sex happens at 3 o'clock in the afternoon while Mom is away at work."[20]

"Babies having babies" have been described in many international studies inspired by the soaring North American rates of teen-age pregnancies. One widely acclaimed study by the New York-based Alan Guttmacher Institute recorded that forty-four out of every 1,000 teen-age girls in Canada becomes pregnant. However, there are astonishing differences in provincial figures. Quebec is reported to have only 25.5 per 1,000, while Alberta and Saskatchewan have the highest percentages, 65 and 62 per cent respectively.[21]

Subsequently, Alberta and Saskatchewan have sponsored province-wide Teen-Aid groups, patterned after American models. Programs are endeavouring to bring back respect for chastity and abstinence, while warning of the dangers of sexually transmitted diseases, and the negative side effects of contraceptives, including their use over a long period of time.

LeAnna Benn, director of Teen-Aid in the United States, believes that divorce, and broken homes generally are the major contributing factors in this crisis situation, "with the kids seeking in early sex the love and security they are no longer getting at home." Such early "heavy" emotional involvement and its consequences are often seen to lead to suicides.[22]

Stanley Henshaw, one of the American sociologists studying the Canadian incidence of teen pregnancy, has pointed out that "Teen-agers in North America are caught in a terrible situation... being told to believe one thing, but in fact, to act another."[23] Feminism and the example of many parents in divorce and subsequent relationships, have already taught them liberation from former restraints.

Meanwhile, the babies of teen-age mothers are often disadvantaged from conception. As a girl's nutritional requirements are greatest in her teen-age years, the fetus must compete with the mother's own growth needs, and this often results in brain and neurological disorders. The physical and emotional immaturity of teen-age mothers could be responsible for defective births. Later, public health authorities must often deal with child abuse and neglect, perpetrated by adolescent mothers, usually out of sheer ignorance and frustration. Some of these mothers, doomed to a life of poverty and welfare dependency, simply become bitter and extremely resentful of the child.[24]

At the same time, gynaecologists across the continent, alarmed at the rising incidence of cervical cancer among teen-age girls, are urging regular Pap tests for girls who are sexually active, as early as 12 years of age.[25]

RUNAWAYS, STREET KIDS, AND CRIME

The desperate plight of runaways who become the teen-age prostitutes on the streets of our large cities, is described in a comprehensive first study, funded by Covenant House, a shelter for such young people, and the United States Justice Department. Dr. Ann Burgess, a University of Pennsylvania professor of psychiatric nursing, and the Reverend Mark-David Janus, chaplain at the University of Connecticut, who conducted the investigations, warn that a large percentage of these children will die of drug overdoses, murder, or suicide, unless government and its social agencies quickly address this urgent problem.[26]

There are more than 10,000 runaways on the streets of Toronto alone, it is estimated. Sixty-three per cent of those interviewed were male and 37 per cent were female, all averaging 17.9 years of age. Forty-six per cent of them revealed that they had run away from home *three times or more*. The study found that 47 per cent had come from single-parent homes, and another significant percentage had been fleeing stepparents.[27]

The Toronto police report that there are 300 known female prostitutes under 18 in the Metro area, and that forty-five between the ages of 12 and 15 were identified between January and July of 1985. Prostitutes as young as 11 have also been picked up in police sweeps.

At the same time, the general crime rate among teen-agers on this continent has risen in some large cities a hundredfold. The teens have been found to be, not the unemployed youth leaving school, but mainly the unhappy, emotionally confused adolescents from all levels of society.

They accounted for 15,000 criminal offences in the city of Toronto in 1984. In the first six months of 1985, there were also 550 criminal charges laid against offenders in Toronto under 12 years of age.

TEEN-AGE SUICIDE

Another damning commentary on our present-day society must be the accelerating rate of suicide among our teen-agers. Statistics indicate that it has become the leading cause of death among teen-agers in Canada today. [28]

The federal task force investigating suicides in Canada, found in its five-year study that the national rate for 15- to 19-year-olds increased 327 per cent between 1965 and 1982. It estimated that the ratio of suicide attempts to suicide completions among this group may be as high as 100 to one. (In the United States, 5,000 to 10,000 American teen-agers take their own lives every year, out of an estimated 500,000 attempts.)

The increase in adolescent suicide rates correlates closely with the breakup of the nuclear family, according to many Canadian and American researchers. Canadian hospital records also reveal that 33 per cent of all the children brought in after attempted suicide are from single-parent families. More than a dozen Canadian children between the ages of five and nine have committed suicide since 1971. [29]

One 15-year-old girl, revived at the Hospital for Sick Children in Toronto, after a suicide attempt, tried to explain: "When Mom divorced Dad, we were going to move into this flashy apartment — but I couldn't take

Spunky — and one day when I was at school, Mom had him put to sleep." Through tears of anguish, she continued, "Every time in my life, when Mom and Dad were fighting, or when I failed in one of my exams [she was actually a solid B student], I would put my arms tightly around Spunky, and nothing would seem too bad...."

Of course, pets have always proven emotional anchors for children, as well as teaching them empathy, kindness, and responsibility. Unfortunately, many modern mothers, presently pursuing two careers, refuse to allot the time or energy to accommodate any pets.

EDUCATION

There are American and Canadian psychiatrists who are beginning to believe that the re-educating of girls and boys into an androgynous mold may contribute to very serious disorientation in future generations. Whether matriarchal theories can be reinforced in the female and male psyches to disregard successfully biology and traditional directions has yet to be proven.[30]

Even toys for the youngest child are now being designed to reverse, or at least traverse, the traditional male and female roles in society. I have heard of little boys finding dolls under their Christmas trees, while little girls are often offered the building sets.

The North York Board of Education brings plumbers and steamfitters into the schools to speak to career development classes for girls. Home economics periods and manual training classes have long since disappeared into an adrogynous blend, with emphasis on the redirection of each sex toward traditionally opposite interests. The little girls who take to hammers like ducks to water, and little boys who become whizzes on the sewing machine, are always the prizewinners.

These trends are underway in varying stages in every

area of education throughout every province in Canada.
In the elementary, junior high, and secondary schools,
there are special classes in mathematics and science for
girls. Meanwhile, incentives, including long-term scholarships, to attract women into the former traditionally male
fields are becoming common at our universities.[31] There
has been a concerted effort to pave the way for more
women to enter the coveted AI (Artificial Intelligence)
degree course.

It may be only a matter of time before women will
dominate all disciplines at Canadian universities, with
female acceptance skyrocketing. At the graduate-school
level between 1973 and 1982, female enrollment increased
90 per cent with male enrollment decreasing four per
cent. By 1982, 59.2 per cent of all master's graduates in
the health professions were women, according to Statistics
Canada. In the 1985-86 university year, female enrollment in pharmacy was 69.9 per cent of the total, which
is considered particularly significant in the business
world, as the majority of drug stores across Canada may
soon be owned or managed by women.[32]

As female numbers gain on or exceed male numbers in
medical schools across the continent, problems with
future matriarchal dominance begin to concern medical
management boards.

The Canadian Medical Association survey of 38,600
members indicated that women choose family practice
more often than the other specialties, predicting that
even by 1992, there could be a serious shortage of
surgeons, radiologists, and other specialists. The CMA
also reported that women working full-time generally
work fewer hours than men and retire earlier. Many are
in part-time practice or are temporarily not practising at
all.

Orville Adams, the CMA's director of medical economics, analyzing the survey in the CMA *Journal*, stated

that the growing number of women graduating is already having an impact on the practice of medicine in Canada, with the number of hours worked annually by the average physician decreasing.

Meanwhile, increasing the number of women on faculties of all our Canadian universities has become a priority. A vice-president of one of our major universities (he refused to be named), says that women are now "consistently chosen for university posts, if their credentials come near those of male applicants. Nowhere is leapfrogging becoming more evident, although William Sayers, among others, a spokesman for the Council of Ontario Universities, has tried to explain that "there is no justified quick way to tenured positions."[33]

Where leapfrogging is positively unfeasible, universities are creating teaching positions for women, led by the University of Western Ontario in London. Queen's University in Kingston, Ontario, with 56 per cent of its undergraduate population now female, has also made the hiring of women faculty members a prime objective, with arbitrary determination to find qualified women to fill ten newly created posts.

Finding qualified applicants of either sex for university teaching positions is often a desperate quest of great consequence at any time. For example, there were 227 university teaching positions in accounting and finance open in North America in the 1985-86 academic year, but only seventeen Ph.D. graduates who could qualify for these positions. Yet all the incentives attracting university undergraduate students into this field seem to address "Women Only."

So, will all little girls be heading in such directions? Certainly, occupations they formerly sought, such as that of "secretary," have been systematically downgraded in career-guidance — almost to the point of extinction. Many young women used to learn to type and file, and entered companies where they learned on the job to organize work and offices to become vital cogs in businesses across the country. Of course, many of them thought of their jobs as probable "short-term" professions, filling in time before they married their "boss" or one of their co-workers. With their double aims in mind, they never demanded top pay, as then, in conscience, they would have to give as much attention, time, and dedication to the firms as the men who were settling into their lifework.

Donald Shaw, president of Shaw Business Colleges in Toronto, which has trained secretaries for ninety-four years, says there are twelve jobs for every secretarial graduate. The president of one of the largest manufacturing companies in Canada says, "We have learned that we must no longer advertise for a secretary, but for an 'administrative assistant.'[34] The feminists have decreed 'secretary' to be a dirty word, as 'homemaker' has become under their rule." He added, "Furthermore, I make the coffee now in my own office, and when we have our sales meetings, we are always careful to ask one of the men to do the honours."

The idea of women serving others in any capacity, in any area of our society, has become taboo.

9

The Story of the Miss Teen Canada Pageant

Canada, the North American continent — the whole world — we must realize, is ultimately in the hands of our children, of our young people. Therefore, paying attention to what they are, where they are, seeing to all their needs, and helping solve their problems today must become our priority, particularly in a transitional society.

That all of them are not in trouble, that an increasing number of them may, indeed, have the vision, strength, and leadership qualities to carry us all beyond the currents in which so many of us presently have lost our footing, became evident in the spring of 1985 in Toronto, when forty cross-country finalists gathered for the seventeenth Annual Miss Teen Canada Pageant and CTV Special.

Suddenly, from coast to coast, Canadians were seeing beyond the stunning physical beauty of our teen-age contestants, to discover "what they are" and "where they are." Their individualism, convictions, and courage were to become far more significant that week of the Pageant than their singing, dancing, bathing suits, and sports spectaculars.

In an astonishing scenario that might have been planned by CTV, as it had all the ingredients of a television thriller — surprise, confrontation, combat — "the girls" were to become headline material, certainly rocking the still-forming foundations of our matriarchal and non-sexist society. There is no doubt that *they made history*, with landmark courage not seen in any other segment of society, as they successfully raised some fascinating new flags.

Actually, it was *The Toronto Star*'s Questionnaire for the Miss Teen Canada contestants, which queried, "Do you consider yourself a feminist?" and "Do you have a role model?" that developed into a major story, on account of their responses and ensuing battles with radical feminists. A series of articles followed in that newspaper, and triggered hundreds of other articles, as well as letters to the editor, and new surveys, in newspapers and magazines across the country.

Basically, their reply to that first question was: "We are *not* feminists." They made such statements as:

> We are who we are. . . . We come from every corner of Canada — *our* Canada of opportunities, opportunities that are not the gift of the Women's Liberation Movement, as Libbers would have us believe — but of our own way of life, our parents and our roots and governments. . . .
>
> We have our own ideas, our own beliefs, our own ambitions. . . .
>
> We intend to be in charge of our own lives, making our own successes, our own mistakes, our own future. . . .
>
> We will not be dictated to, or organized, or led by the nose into a way of life that we now see as highly undesirable. . . .

As *Toronto Star* columnists Lynda Hurst and Doris Anderson were probably the most vocally militant feminists in the country at that time, "the girls" might have expected the torrents of scorn and abuse in ensuing *Toronto Star* articles. They were mercilessly belittled as "mindless,"[1] with their biggest problems, "the appearance of a pimple, the disappearance of a date, or in this case, the winning of an inane beauty contest."

In a scathing response to one identified contestant, Lynda Hurst said: "Now, I realize I'm not dealing with a doctoral scholar here...."[2] In truth, she might have been dealing with a future doctoral scholar, as the intellectual abilities of the contestants were tested and proven above average.

From towns and cities across Canada, sponsored by their own communities and commercial enterprises, they had come to vie for the $100,000 in prizes, and the honour and glamour of becoming Miss Teen Canada, Miss Teen Fitness, and Miss Teen Friendship, as well as competing for three special Britannica scholastic awards. While few of them, at an average age of 17, presumed they could win in any category, they had looked forward to having the experience of travelling to a big city, and of making new friends from other towns and provinces, an invaluable and unifying element of the Pageant, according to the sponsors.

They also had the opportunity of appearing on national television, which required professional dance instruction for the choreographed numbers. There was a crash course in professional make-up, dressing, and general deportment — "finishing school," one girl called it.

The learning experience they could not have foreseen was the avalanche of disapproval that poured forth on their heads in the media after they dared to express their non-feminist opinions. Nor could they have realized that such views had been effectively silenced by powerful feminist militants in all media for more than two decades.

They may not have been old enough to remember the violence of the feminists who disrupted the Miss Canada Pageant of November 3, 1975, that sent one studio guard to hospital with broken ribs.[3] Nor would they have heard of the bomb threats that Lionel Tiger, an anthropologist at the University of British Columbia, was reported to be receiving in 1978 before his public lectures. He was questioning the feminist theory that "most of the differences between men and women were purely the result of cultural patterning."[4] When his book, *Men in Groups*, was featured in a cover story in *Maclean's*, feminists picketed the magazine.

Incidentally, Lionel Tiger was not the only scientist at that time attempting to explain the differences in male and female behaviour as a result of biological factors, rather than "the outcome of coercive social institutions, legal and religious precepts and psychological conditioning," as was preached by the revolutionary feminists. June Reinisch of Rutgers University in New Jersey was publishing her research indicating that the amount of male and female hormones a fetus receives affects the socio-sexual development of a boy or a girl,[5] while Sandra Witelson of McMaster University in Hamilton, Ontario, had accumulated data showing that the right and left hemispheres of the brain tend to develop at different rates and with different emphasis in males and females, with the result that there are certainly differences in the way males and females "process information."[6]

Even if the Miss Teen Canada contestants had been warned of the possible repercussions, it is unlikely that they would have been intimidated, as eleven of them were to throw themselves further into the fray with a blistering letter to their attackers on *The Toronto Star*. "We did not appreciate your comments regarding that only a handful of us 'appear to have grown up in the same world as the rest of us,'" they wrote. "Feminist groups in this country support issues which many of us young and grownups of the future do not support. To us, feminists do not represent the women of today. They are a minority of vocal troublemakers and therefore, our group wouldn't ever want to associate with them. . . ." They added fat to the fire with, "We also think the media should take blame for the lack of morality in our society."[7]

Teen-agers against seasoned 40- to 60-year-old feminists and powerful publications such as *The Toronto Star* may have seemed an unequal battle, but in less than a month, there appeared an amazing revelation in the media — that the Miss Teen Canada contestants may simply have been speaking out for the majority of teen-age girls across the country.

It came to light that as far back as January 1985, the Newsletter of the Ontario Advisory Council on Women's Issues, under the new president, Sam Ion, had reported, indeed, that "there are few feminists under the age of 35":

> Young girls are not yet aware of the inequalities in the current system. Everybody makes the same wage at 16 — minimum wage! The pressure is still strong for girls to drop maths and sciences, thus eliminating the vast array of jobs of the future. Although they can see alternate paths of home, family or a career, they can't seem to envision a viable combination.
>
> We *must* reach these young women before they reach 30, before they discover that in order to be what they've decided they would like to be they have to go back and get their Grade 12 physics or geometry! It's discouraging at that late date and might just keep a lot of them in a job ghetto.
>
> We need ideas, programs, practical suggestions as to how to reach them. Perhaps each and every women's group in the province can 'adopt' one teen-

age girl *and* her mother (her strongest influence) and expand their educational expectations and horizons.[8]

With the millions of dollars available to Women's Councils across the country, instituting campaigns and surveys is never a problem. While the Ontario Advisory Council geared up for this crisis, the federal Canadian Advisory Council on the Status of Women, indicating its alarm at the statements of the Miss Teen Canada contestants, in April 1985 made public its 166-page study of 150 adolescents from the ages of 15 to 19, covering five provinces, that also revealed a marked absence of feminist goals.[9]

The study found that the majority of teen-age girls still had "rosy" dreams of being married, having loving husbands, trouble-free children, and home ownership, nor did they anticipate divorce in their lives. Half of them expected to be the principal homemakers, doing most of the housework, although some of them would relegate "drying the supper dishes to husbands." There were girls who sought to marry men with the kinds of jobs that would improve their lifestyles, but many said it did not matter what the man's occupation was, "as long as they loved each other." Most of the twenty-eight boys included in the study had matching expectations, visualizing their wives in charge of the home and the raising of children.

Only 20 per cent of the girls wanted to pursue careers as lawyers, professors, doctors, or diplomats, a percentage that seemed to surprise interviewers. While most of the others might work in traditionally female occupations, before and after marriage, none of them expressed concern over the penalties for absence in producing children, nor were they concerned over the lack of day care.

Maureen Baker, an Ottawa sociologist in charge of the project, concluded that these findings mirrored the very conservative, unrealistic viewpoint of mothers of another generation. "In the eyes of these adolescents, there is no unemployment in their futures, no divorce, and no poverty," the study reported, demanding that adolescents be brought up to date with a more realistic approach to the problems of modern times. (They might have said matriarchal times.)

"The romanticized versions of the future we received in the interviews are partly a factor of the adolescents' inexperience in the world.... But they can be blamed partly on the lack of time and energy that our society as a whole ...puts into preparing young women for a drastically altered society," was the general conclusion, and it accused the schools that shied away from controversy for failing to provide the necessary information to young people, especially teen-age girls.

Doris Anderson, in *The Toronto Star*, then asked in headlines, "Why Should Young Girls Live a Fairy Tale?" She reported on another study that also apparently alarmed the feminists. Conducted by Dr. Gloria Geller at the University of Regina, it involved 400 girls in Grades 9, 12 and 13, in six schools, three in Toronto and three in Regina. These girls had expressed, in diaries, aspirations and expectations very similar to those recorded in the Ottawa study.

Almost 75 per cent of these girls intended to go into traditional occupations, nursing, teaching, or secretarial science, "although many of those traditional jobs won't exist because of technology in ten years," Mrs. Anderson insisted. (How anyone could presume that such jobs will ever be obsolete, in any society, is certainly a conundrum.)

"Isn't it sad that girls can't be prepared to cope better with what's really ahead for them? Why do we put them through a living fairy tale again and again, before they are wakened up with a jolt?" Mrs. Anderson pointed out that many of the girls have divorced parents and single mothers, and yet they would not face up to the fact that divorce could happen to them. (The Miss Teen Canada contestants had retorted, heatedly, "that it was not a foregone conclusion that it would happen to them!") "Girls are being raised to expect a traditional way of life that vanished for most women 20 years ago."[10]

It vanished for those women who had wholeheartedly espoused the Women's Liberation Movement, but the question of how many women, especially mothers, never did espouse the Cause now arises. They were legion, according to their daughters, as it became evident that the Miss Teen Canada contestants were speaking out for a significant number of teen-age girls throughout the country, influenced by mothers and still attracted to "a traditional way of life."

Commenting on the Anderson article, one teen-age girl wrote:

> If that kind of world the old feminists would hand down to us — condemns us to divorce, single parenthood, and lonely old age, well, then, are you surprised that we say NO, NO, NO, to feminism, and try to reverse the trends? We think Women's Lib has produced many of those miserable conditions — driving a wedge between men and women. . . .

Many contestants and other teen-agers were to write letters describing their mothers, such as:

> My mother is a doctor with an office in the house. She has always been there when we needed her. She is not a feminist.

> My mother and father own a store and my mother works on the books, sometimes in the store and sometimes at home, and we kids help in the store on Saturdays. Mom is not a feminist because she says she does not believe in affirmative action. The store clerks are all men and have been with Mom and

Dad for years and years. The women they used to employ and don't want to employ again were always rushing off to take their kids to appointments, or leaving to get married a few months after they were trained to handle the equipment.

My mother is an artist and was offered a teaching position at Art College before she decided to marry Dad and be a forester's wife in our far northern town. Now she designs quilts and shows them at exhibitions, even in the States. She says if she had been a feminist she would have stayed in the city and missed Dad and us and all those prizes she wins with her quilts!

My mother is a single mother who left Dad to go back to work, but my brother and I believe she has regretted it ever since. She makes more money now than my father did, and we have a great apartment, lots of clothes and trips, and she is a kind and wonderful mother. Still, she works so hard she never makes friends — and she doesn't laugh much. I think she's a lonely feminist.

I suppose you would call my mother an "ordinary" housewife — but what is an "ordinary" housewife? We sure don't have much money, and Mom works like a slave for Dad and us kids — but she is always singing. Dad calls her "Boss" or "Queenie," and she certainly orders us around. But you couldn't be unhappy for long around Mom — she's constantly planning something to look forward to, like birthdays, or picnics — Mom says she could never be a feminist and work outside the home because she "wouldn't have time to watch the birds outside the kitchen window."[11]

Any small-town newspaper editor who asked for comments from teen-age girls on the cross-Canada kerfuffle was almost overwhelmed by the response. The Miss Teen Canada contestants' courage had loosed all their tongues, inspiring courage to express their own opinions, but, of greater importance perhaps, eventually to make their own individual and unique choices of lifestyles, considering all options.

"Feminists have been dictators — imposing their theories and way of life on others," they repeated.

We will *not* be dictated to . . . we have *the Right* to dream our own dreams, make our own decisions — without their interference. If some of us would rather be teachers and nurses and secretaries than engineers — why should they force us into physics — when our brothers and boyfriends *want* physics and are able to fill the corresponding jobs. Any girl with an aptitude and desire for physics is welcome to it — and she hasn't needed to be pushed and favoured to pass it. . . . What we really don't understand is why feminists are so determined to drive all the men into the kitchen to do the cooking and into the nursery to look after the kids — and turn all the girls into Rosie the Riveter.

We girls want to be considered as "persons," not segregated off into a corner of the ring as "Women's-Libbers," who come out punching and clawing against the men at every imagined inequality. . . . Men are not *our* enemies. We love our fathers, our grandfathers, our brothers and our boyfriends, and *we* still believe in *ordinary* happy marriages, in spite of those divorce statistics — which we blame on the Women's Liberation Movement.

Girls in the smaller centres consistently disagreed with

the articles and statistics that tried to prove that a traditional way of life had vanished for most women twenty years ago.

The Miss Teen Canada contestants who wrote the joint letter to *The Toronto Star* also counterattacked feminist political demands. They stated:

> We do not believe in equal pay for work of equal value, but we believe in equal pay for equal work.[12]

Others wrote:

> We do not think that Prime Minister Mulroney or our own provincial government leaders are unfair in not giving in to all those women's-libbers who want a lot of things other Canadian women do not want. The women's-libbers want everyone to believe that they speak for all Canadian women — *but they do not.* They simply cannot force all Canadian women into one giant mold.

Militant Canadian feminists have certainly attempted to coerce women across the country into a political bloc, but so far have experienced the same resistance as that recorded on the American scene. During the 1984 presidential election, the majority of women voted for Ronald Reagan, turning down the Democrats' vice-presidential candidate, Geraldine Ferraro, and the sweeping feminist causes enshrined in ERA (the Equal Rights Amendment). The most notable Canadian attempt, of course, and a major achievement by the Canadian Action Committee on the Status of Women, was the *Women's Debate*, during the 1984 Canadian federal election. In a nationwide telecast, militant feminist panelists demanded that party leaders Brian Mulroney, John Turner, and Ed Broadbent state their platforms on women's issues, threatening them with an *en bloc* female vote.

Teen-agers across Canada were obviously watching that performance, but also there were women across the country, as well as men, who were writhing with the leaders at the matriarchal tone of the proceedings. Geills Turner, wife of the Liberal leader, said, "I feel a little patronized, because these issues are being debated separately by women."[13] Maureen Sabia, a Toronto lawyer, complained later on the CBC's *Journal*, "It is time for women to move out of the ghetto of feminism into the larger world, achieving a place there because of merit, not because they belong to a particular sex."

Columnist Dennis Braithwaite, in *The Toronto Sun*, called the Debate "phony, unreal, unfair, uncalled-for and basically silly," and he, like "the girls," also believed that the feminists were not representing Canadian women.

> Women have grievances (who hasn't?), but most of them realize that the solution doesn't lie in badgering the governments for handouts, special treatment or a means to punish men. Real women are sensible. They are for peace and against injustice in any form. They are not sex-obsessed, and they don't believe that the only way to rise is by putting somebody down.[14]

Political analyst and columnist Dalton Camp, who likened the Debate to a "re-run of the match between the Christians and the lions (for the record, the lions won)," was convinced that only in Toronto could there be such an event. "There just isn't any place in this broad land of ours other than the Queen City where you'd find so many women assembled in one room so unrepresentative of the attitudes and the sensibilities of their sex," he claimed.[15]

This observation of Dalton Camp's illuminates the story of the Miss Teen Canada Pageant, as it suggests that the hotbeds of militant feminism are mainly to be found in large cities, such as Toronto and New York, leaving smaller centres less affected by the Women's Liberation Movement. This could account for the anti-feminist sentiments of the Miss Teen Canada contestants, as they were primarily from the smaller centres. Indeed, many of them saw their home towns as unimpressed and largely unaffected by the feminist revolution.

I recall, as well, that at the Judy LaMarsh Memorial Dinner, held during the Liberal leadership convention in the spring of 1984, Laurie Talmey, the National Liberal Women's Committee president, insisted that Liberal women vote *en bloc* for the candidate who would best serve their interests. That proposal was defeated by the eloquent resistance of two delegates from smaller centres in New Brunswick, Dr. Marilyn Trenholm, a riding association president from Sackville, and Rachel Bannister, an insurance agent from Shediac. Senator Lorna Marsden, chairman of the Liberal National Policy Committee, and Iona Campagnolo, the party president, joined them in objecting to women's being split off into a special interest group.

Nellie McClung, even in her earliest endeavours for suffrage, always vehemently opposed the creation of a "Women's Party" that would deal primarily with women's issues. Neither would she have accommodated the "liberation" in the modern Women's Movement, as she steadfastly preached traditional family values and the "centrality of the maternal experience." She simply believed that women's vote from the workplace or the fireside was their ultimate equality.

Veronica Strong-Boag, in an introduction to Nellie McClung's book, *In Times Like These*, wrote: "She failed, as did the majority of American feminists, to provide modern women with satisfactory identity models...in a newly secular world and an increasingly permissive society...."[16]

However, teen-age Canadian girls have said that they see Nellie McClung herself, as a "satisfactory identity model" — an immensely strong family figure, as well as a reformer of her society — in no way resembling the feminists of today.

In fact, many of the Miss Teen Canada contestants were ready for *The Toronto Star*'s question: "Do you have a role model?" with some of their answers again causing consternation in feminist ranks.

ROLE MODELS

To the question, "Do you have a role model?" the majority of contestants replied: "My mother," but other role models named repeatedly were Mother Teresa, Anne Murray, and Mila Mulroney. Furthermore, these same answers occurred again and again in a flood of letters to the editors of local newspapers, written by inspired teen-agers across the country.

Unfortunately, the wrath of militant media feminists, once more aroused at such an unlikely list, would glance off "the girls," resulting in a direct, bombarding assault on the most visible role model — Mila Mulroney — an assault that seriously backfired on the Women's Liberation Movement in Canada.

Miss Teen Ottawa-Hull, Shellagh Stronach, explained her choice of role model: "Mila Mulroney... I feel she is a model woman who represents our identity in the 80s."[17] Mila Mulroney's beauty, background, education, and decisions had been the subject of hundreds of articles following her husband's election as Prime Minister of Canada, articles, apparently, that made the deepest impression on teen-age girls across the country.

Everyone knew that she is the daughter of an immigrant doctor, that she grew up in Montreal, and had been a civil engineering student, aiming toward architecture when she married Brian Mulroney, a Montreal lawyer ten years her senior. He was the son of an electrician from Baie Comeau on the North Shore of the St. Lawrence. She continued with her studies for only two and a half years, until she was seven months pregnant with her second child, and three subjects short of her engineering degree. "A good marriage and motherhood are worth all the degrees you can get,"[18] she told one interviewer.

"I'm very old-fashioned about marriage," she has said, repeatedly. "Brian comes first with me, always. We are best friends. We are a partnership."[19] (An unbeatable political partnership, as well, according to Allan Fotheringham, *Maclean's* columnist, who wrote: "Mulroney admits — and it's a true fact, he never would have been elected without her," claiming that she was "a great national campaigner who can work a room better than Lyndon Johnson or Milton Berle!")

Mila Mulroney has also repeatedly indicated how strongly she feels about raising her children herself — that she may have occasional help with the children, but would never employ a "nanny." She and the Prime Minister spend most of their private time with their children, seeking to give them security in an old-fashioned family life, patterned after the ones they themselves experienced.

That Mila Mulroney now must defend her dedication to marriage and motherhood, and her own choice of a traditional lifestyle, to feminists, is surely a phenomenon of a matriarchy.

"Mila may dust and scrub and be a good cook...but she is obviously not an ordinary homemaker, any more than I'm the Queen of Sheba," Lois Sweet attacked her in *The Toronto Star.* Under the headline, "Mila Undermines the Choices of Working Mothers," this columnist cited Mila's myriad duties as the wife of the Prime Minister, with her own parliamentary office processing the hundreds of invitations that come in weekly. She accused the

Prime Minister's wife of "pretending," and wrote, "What Mila Mulroney does, after all, carries considerable political import. She is in a very powerful position and could use it for the benefit of others besides herself."[20]

The Globe and Mail did not question her integrity, as had the Lois Sweet article, but it took the Prime Minister's pet name for his wife to use in a mocking front-page headline. "Teddy Bear Mila Mulroney Wears Diamonds, Does Sinks." Still, the loving, caring image of a teddy bear was captured in the ensuing newspaper article, with Janis Johnson, a national Conservative Party director, pointing out, "It's a long time since Canadians have seen a loving family in Sussex Drive."[21]

Maclean's quoted *The Toronto Star* columnist Doris Anderson as saying, "Mila Mulroney is a throwback to my mother's day, like the beauty pageants and other things that are still around — just 'quaint.'"

The feminists were pulling out all stops, perhaps without realizing that Mila Mulroney was already entrenched, generally, in public affections.

A teen-age girl in Chiliwack wrote: "If Mila Mulroney is 'quaint' then every teen-age girl I know would like to be 'quaint.'"

In a cross-country survey, other teen-agers also expressed admiration for Geills Turner, wife of the federal Opposition Leader. She has a Harvard graduate degree in business, and was a systems engineer with IBM in Montreal, before she gave up that profession for home-making and motherhood. "Two careers infringe on the time you need with your kids,"[22] she has reiterated positively, and although her children are older than the Mulroneys', she still considers herself a full-time mother, in addition to taking on the duties of an Opposition Leader's wife. (One Miss Teen Canada contestant was visiting in Vancouver when Geills Turner and her daughter knocked on the door seeking Turner votes. She is convinced that it was Mrs. Turner and Elizabeth who saved that riding for the Opposition Leader.) Having gained her degrees and job and made her choices long before the feminist revolution, Geills Turner, among thousands of other women on this continent, must also wonder now why they must answer to the feminists.

There is no doubt that the lifestyles of the women and their families presently in the political limelight in Ottawa and the provincial capitals may be having considerable influence among teen-agers.

Even Lucille Broadbent, wife of Ed Broadbent, leader of the federal New Democrats, whose party champions many tenets of the Women's Liberation Movement, is noted for her old-fashioned influence. A teacher and widow for six years before marrying the NDP leader in 1971, her charm, warmth, and experience are said to have resulted in her becoming a "mother-confessor" to many young Ottawa wives. While some of them, in their 20s and 30s, have gone back to the universities and take their studies extremely seriously, she has suggested that "their marriages should still come first. If a marriage is in jeopardy, and a wife has to choose between work on an essay and attending a constituency affair, she should choose the social event,"[23] she is quoted as stating.

Lucille Broadbent has also drawn young Ottawa political wives into the Parliamentary Wives' Association, whose remarkable committee work on human rights, under presidents Jane Crosbie and Penny Collenette, has been recognized at home and abroad. As close friendships develop among party wives, as they do in all volunteer organizations, these women and their high-profile group may be leading younger generations of women back to volunteer work, removing the feminist stigma that deemed all unpaid effort "unworthy."

Flora MacDonald is apparently another great favourite among young people, a fact that may have influenced Prime Minister Mulroney in appointing her federal Minister of Employment (in charge of youth training programs). Of course, she gained "heroine" status among young people when she became internationally famous as the cabinet Minister for External Affairs in Joe Clark's administration, with her department and the Canadian Embassy in Tehran organizing the escape of the American hostages from Iran.

Flora MacDonald has been called the role model for the girls who stay single, and single-minded, some of whom may have her dedication to politics. A Cape Breton native, at 58 she has had twenty-eight years of political experience in Ottawa, beginning as a secretary in the Conservative Party headquarters. She is known to be an incredibly hard worker who often sleeps overnight in her government office during hectic work sessions.

However, it has now become clear, according to all the studies that have followed the Miss Teen Canada Pageant, that a significant number of teen-age girls in Canada have decided that marriage and motherhood are their priorities. (They may still be brainwashed into deciding on other futures in the Women's Courses at our universities.) Not that they rule out the possibilities of springboarding from the family experience into later political involvement, as that would seem to be the pattern of the majority of our women M.P.'s today. It is a pattern that suggests that there is a special timing for most women entering politics, perhaps coming from family and community experiences.

Naturally, many "glamour" figures have their impact on impressionable teen-agers, such as Anne Murray (whom they also see as a happily married woman, devoted to her children). There is no way to gauge the influence of their favourite movie star, Brooke Shields, with her avowal to "remain a virgin until she marries." She may have been leading thousands of young people away from "liberation" and promiscuity on both sides of the border.

NON-ROLE MODELS

Even if the Miss Teen Canada contestants and their contemporaries do fall into the Women's Courses at our universities, it is unlikely that they will ever discover any "satisfactory identity models" among the original feminists in the Women's Liberation Movement, whose works will be compulsory study.

The Feminine Mystique, the book that launched the Women's Liberation Movement on this continent, they will consider "out of date," and the famous author herself certainly no role model. Divorced and living alone, Betty Friedan lectures on the need to replace traditional relationships with "new family groupings," her own unique suggestion for sharing, for defeating loneliness. In 1978, she was asking, "Why is my own daughter so defensive, so embarrassed about the Women's Movement, about feminism?" and she has described her distress when one of her sons blamed some of his personal problems on the Women's Movement.[24]

They will read *The Second Sex,* by Simone de Beauvoir, who became a failure in her own eyes. The author was editing the Marxist Review, *Les Temps Modernes,* with her live-in companion, philosopher Jean-Paul Sartre, in Paris when she wrote her brilliant thesis endeavouring to demonstrate that woman was always simply considered in her relation to man. Woman, she said, was therefore continually forced into an inferior position, to be "subjugated by man." When the book was translated into English in 1953, reviewers admired its scope and the author's insight, but warned that it should be accepted only in its socialist context.

In 1985, Simone de Beauvoir was questioning her own doctrines. "I abdicated womanhood to become a class collaborationist," she explained, and women following in her footsteps, she believed, "are no better off today." Resulting "male aggressiveness and hostility, and much more rape, have become so common that no woman feels at ease in Paris,"[25] she was regretting, in interviews shortly before her death.

Kate Millett, known as "the Triumphant Lesbian," whose book, *Sexual Politics*, published in 1970, was temporarily to eclipse all other feminist literature, was the most influential leader of the Gay Rights Group in NOW, the National Organization of Women in the United States. In 1971, she was dominating the organization when it passed resolutions recognizing "the double oppression of lesbians," and endorsing "child custody rights to mothers who are lesbians," with homosexuals across the continent reaping the benefits. Now a shadowy figure, she is no role model. She is an accomplished sculptor, acclaimed for her latest work, a girl's corpse — with the face of Kate Millett.

Non-feminists and feminists alike, as well as younger women who may be seeking role models, have registered revulsion at the lifestyle of Germaine Greer, whose book, *The Female Eunuch*, published in 1970, was an examination of sexual relations, in which woman's role as a sex object required a passivity that actually made her a female "eunuch." This beautiful Australian, usually described as an "Amazon" in intellect as well as in physical stature, became perhaps the most famous proponent, worldwide, of the "liberation" of women.

She studied for her doctorate at Cambridge, and was teaching in England when she began her dazzling series of lectures throughout Europe and America, insisting that women must cast off "the shackles of marriage, family and sexual repression." She herself provided the example, posing nude for the pornographic magazine *Suck*, and flaunting her numerous short-lived relationships, two of them with convicted men of known violence, in which she suffered three abortions, and finally a disastrous, well-publicized marriage that lasted three weeks.

Germaine Greer in the 1980s is preaching a different

message in her book, *Sex and Destiny: The Politics of Human Feritility,* and on the talk show circuit. She sees a "sterile decadence in western societies," and warns of "the slow suicide of her own culture." She contends that the liberated, permissive western community that she was advocating fifteen years ago is now obviously "sliding toward extinction." In almost an about-face, she retracts earlier premises, and lauds motherhood and children, repeating over and over, "Most of the pleasure in the world is still provided by children and not by genital dabbling." In the United States and Canada, she denounces what she understands as a particularly North American trend toward women's "careerism," calling it a "facet of child-hating."[26]

Many now view Germaine Greer as a tragic figure, self-doubting, and often viciously attacked by feminists she formerly led, while the critics are beginning to dismiss her as "she wails over her own failures." She long ago lost all credibility as a role model, even for committed, "liberated" feminists.

While the New York author, Susan Brownmiller, became famous in the Women's Liberation Movement in 1975 with her book, *Against Our Will,* which dealt with man's subjugation of woman through rape, her latest book, *Femininity,* while reviewed at great length in the world press, seems to be simply distancing her from most women, young and old.

She claims that she spent more than four years researching the subject to come to the conclusion that femininity is nothing more than a snare and a delusion. "Women's sickening and pervasive preoccupation" with being feminine is a "subjugation of themselves," she argues, and is a superficial pursuit based on packaging, which is "a mind-boggling waste of time and energy." However, the author frankly admits that she "slicks up" for the talk shows. She also speaks freely of her "strategic" love affairs in her efforts to forward her career, "one with a legislator," and of her current relationship with a carpenter-writer in New York City. There is confusion in her arguments trying to prove that femininity is actually a camouflage, an art form that uses illusion and imposes incredible limitations. They appear to be falling on deaf ears. [27]

As Canadian feminists attack Mila Mulroney for her non-feminist lifestyle, Susan Brownmiller attacks Nancy Reagan, the American President's wife, and Diana Ross for having "the feminine act down pat with their careful coifs and clothes," very unpopular observations, as those two women, like Mila Mulroney, are entrenched in public affection. Susan Brownmiller could be the last person on earth the Miss Teen Canada contestants would choose for a role model.

While little is known about the lives and times of our own Canadian leaders in the Women's Liberation Movement, the lives and times of these most famous feminists have become common knowledge. To most young people, these particular women appear to be "failures," failures in all their relationships with men — in their marriages, in their understanding, in their accommodation of "the other half of the population."

In fact, if these women and their lives represent the Women's Liberation Movement, does anyone really wonder why the Miss Teen Canada contestants would say "NO, NO, NO," to feminism, and choose "Mother, Anne Murray, Mother Teresa, and Mila Mulroney," as their role models?

Furthermore, could the Canadian federal and provincial governments not find anything better to do with our Canadian tax dollars than spend them on Women's Courses in our universities, where the lives and *thoughts* of such women are studied and, possibly, *followed?*

How can we not be grateful to the courageous Miss Teen Canada contestants, to CTV-Television for bringing them to Toronto, and to *The Toronto Star* for that unique, probing Questionnaire with the answers from our next generation, that may, at least, point us all toward other thoughts.

It is possible that the story of the Miss Teen Canada Pageant of 1985 could find its way, eventually, into Canadian history books.

10
Betty Friedan: The Beginning and the Ending

Most women in the United States and Canada would agree, I believe, that the beginning of the Women's Liberation Movement for them, as for me, was the reading of Betty Friedan's book *The Feminine Mystique*. However, it would be the militant feminists determined to convince us of the oppression in the so-called patriarchy who would run with the ball. I am now quite convinced that they would carry it far, far afield of the future that Betty Friedan herself had envisioned for all of us.

Attending her winter lectures in the spring of 1985 at the University of Florida, I was dismayed that it was a new edition of *The Feminine Mystique* that was being hawked outside the lecture theatres, rather than the author's much later book, *The Second Stage*. In the latter she is constantly straining her awesome writing skills to reconcile her original thesis with the direction and effects of the Women's Liberation Movement across the continent, and throughout our lives.

That she herself was simply swept along in the wake of

the revolutionary tides, often as powerless as the weakest, most vulnerable little housewife, became plain, in her series of articles collected into her second book, *It Changed My Life*.

It changed her life in all aspects, certainly, from the grass-roots anguish of her divorce and broken home, to the exultation she experienced from her own "personal consciousness-raising,"[1] and the "transforming transcendent actions of the Movement." However, "I feel a terrible responsibility," she was writing even then; "We ordinary American women, finding the power to change our lives, changed the face of history."[2]

In the earliest days, as she attacked the "sex objects, mindless household drudges devoted to cleaning the sink,"[3] specifically as seen on television, she received hundreds of vituperative letters accusing her of being an enemy of motherhood, and of destroying the family, but later she would retaliate with stories of these same women letter-writers being won over to the Mystique theory, and returning to jobs or going back to school themselves.[4]

Betty Friedan was incensed when the editors of *The Ladies' Home Journal* decided against using her "new image," that of "a double-headed woman, a strong woman's face emerging from the vapid one," on the cover of a feminist issue, substituting instead the traditional pretty "feminine" model.[5]

As the Movement swept across the continent, she would be riding high and mighty as a Valkyrie on the ship's bow — charting the course, leading the way, setting the rules, perhaps drunk with power, and not seeing the shoals. Yet, if the American feminists had given this honest, deeply sensitive, and brilliant woman their absolute trust, rather than supporting the violently radical protagonists, bent on the immediate destruction of the so-called patriarchal society, I have come to believe, the Women's Liberation Movement might have developed into an evolutionary event with more positive results. Instead it became the revolution that has successfully shattered the lives of men, women, and children throughout the western world.

Betty Friedan has been honest in telling "where she came from," and what shaped her philosophy. During the depression in Peoria, where she grew up, only the men teachers were hired (a first mark against a so-called patriarchy); she felt deeply her mother's unhappiness in a thwarted career and confinement in homemaking and motherhood; she obviously regretted giving up a prestigious fellowship, and eventually her independence, for love, marriage, and motherhood; she would later rage at losing a job because she was several months pregnant; subsequently, she was constantly torn with indecision, waffling backwards and forwards between two worlds.

She failed to look beyond her own frustrations to see the thousands of other similarly talented women who were already successfully accommodating a home life and a work life outside their homes in a democratic society. Of greater significance was the fact that she also failed to see that the majority of middle-class western women were reasonably content in lives of creative homemaking and motherhood.

Her great error, and I believe, a historic tragedy, was her assumption that all those homemakers were experiencing her frustrations. With her magnificent rhetoric, she would be able to persuade them that they were disadvantaged in a world ruled by men, that they were oppressed, and misused, that they were "unfulfilled," that in "raising their consciousness," they would discover all their latent talents and skills that could be cultivated to lead them toward vastly more satisfying lives. Many women who implicitly accepted this premise rearranged their lives accordingly, often with disastrous results.

Later, those women would read Simone de Beauvoir and Shulamith Firestone to learn that motherhood too was nothing but enslavement, the "female trap."

Betty Friedan was apologizing for the power in her rhetoric (which she could not have foreseen), when she wrote in *The Second Stage*, "I resorted to a rather extreme metaphor at that time, likening the 'trap' of the suburban housewife to a 'comfortable concentration camp.'"[6] Again and again, she has also pointed out that *The Statement of Purpose of NOW* (the National Organization of Women), that she drafted, demanded "full equality for women, in truly equal partnership with men," but it forswore "enmity to men."

As hate and vengeance against men were fanned across the continent by the radicals in the Women's Liberation Movement, and highlighted in exaggerated cover stories in *Time* and *Newsweek,* Betty Friedan was writing of being "shocked and outraged" by the extremist voices: "That's not what we meant, not at all."[7] However, she admitted later that her objections had not been loud enough. "We were intimidated by the conformities of the Movement and the reality of 'sisterhood is powerful,'" she wrote.

Besides, she had become the most famous woman in America (she may become known as the most influential woman in all world history), and it would be hard to get off the "glory" road. Originally the very symbol of the Women's Liberation Movement, she worked tirelessly day and night, for NOW, of which she was the principal founder in 1966, organizing chapters across the country, lobbying governments, and raising the funds for numerous lawsuits that would succeed in forging feminist principles.

No longer would an employer who needed a truck driver, or a yard man who could lift 60-pound cartons all day, be able to advertise in a "Help Wanted — Male" column of any newspaper. NOW also fought against the "protective" legislation prohibiting women from lifting more than thirty-five pounds. They won their cases against companies that refused to hire women for traditionally male work, such as telephone linemen and railroad workers. NOW fought so-called sexism in every segment of society, achieving victory after victory, in such issues as the banning of segregated living accommodations on college campuses across the country.

It was when the socialist and lesbian elements began to dominate the Movement that Betty Friedan turned on the radicals, locking horns in conflict after confict, to prevent NOW from being fragmented into warring sects, away from the central issues.

She never faltered in her determination that massive social changes would be brought about within the American democratic system, rather than through a violent socialist upheaval, such as that demanded by such anti-capitalist groups within NOW as the Young Socialist Alliance (YSA), a branch of the Socialist Workers' Party. State socialism, she argued heatedly, would be authoritarian and still full of inequalities.[8]

She fought the lesbian influence with even greater vigour in NOW, as meeting after meeting was taken over by lesbians, such as Kate Millett. They believed lesbianism to be the "only fully feminist position," and demanded that all NOW members affirm this concept publicly. Betty Friedan, who described homosexuality as "spreading like a murky smog over the American scene," in The Feminine Mystique, refused to make such an affirmation as president of NOW in 1970. After she resigned from the presidency in 1971, exhausted from all the battles she had been waging with the radicals, NOW passed all the lesbian resolutions.

Many claim that her purpose in supporting further lesbian proposals ensuring sexual preference at the 1977 National Women's Conference in Houston, Texas, was to heal the internal divisions that threatened NOW's extinction.

Still, by 1981, in *The Second Stage,* she was wondering if the increasing numbers of young men practicing sodomy "has less to do with changes in sexual preference than a new male focus on self-fulfillment and personal growth." She quotes her sociology colleagues at Columbia University, who were studying "Sex Roles and Social Change," who confirmed her impression (while pointing out that there is no data base) of "young men moving to homosexuality or celibacy," simply as an alternative to marriage. This is "the complaint of young women in their peer group. . . the culture of narcissism."[9]

Always affirming that men must be understood and considered, and that it is imperative that they become equal partners in the new society, the author, in chapter after chapter of *The Second Stage*, deals with a multitude of male problems resulting from the radical pell-mell advances of the Women's Liberation Movement.

She writes of the young men married to successful career women who completely subordinate their own ambitions to their wives' wishes, losing all their own drive and competitive spirit (the drive and competitive spirit that built the great industries of America).

She tells the story of one such young man in Chicago who turned down night work and weekend assignments for home responsibilities, allowing his wife to attend law school. His "puzzled boss" decides: "That man isn't going very far. Too bad. He was the pick of the litter."[10]

Another of her stories is of a young man who says: "Becoming a daddy has become very important to me. Why shouldn't she support the family for a while and let *me* find myself?"[11]

In her University of Florida lecture, Betty Friedan tried to convince "The New Man," the subject of her most popular lecture, of all his advantages in the new lifestyles. "He may soon gain a much longer life span," she claimed, as he sloughs off that "masculinity-oriented" drive, and "macho-ness" that formerly produced the stress and heart attacks; and he would become as important to his children as their mother — he would carry them around in a "backpack." (I heard her use this expression a dozen times, "Daddy with the baby in a backpack" — a sight that is to become as common, I presume, as mother with the baby in her womb, or at her breast.)

Yet, in *The Second Stage*, she is questioning: "Are men and women moving in opposite directions, chasing illusions of liberation by simply reversing roles that the other sex has already found imprisoning?"[12]

She quotes another young man: "Every guy I know is in trouble. They can't seem to get it together. They don't know what they want. Only the women seem to be getting it together now."[13]

There are women who are "getting it together." Nevertheless, I see Betty Friedan worrying, as much as some of the rest of us, about the problems of the millions of other women (hundreds in the sociological studies, and hundreds we know personally) who are not "getting it together."

"I sense something *off*, out of focus, going wrong. . . . I've begun to hear undertones of pain and puzzlement, a queasiness, an uneasiness, almost a bitterness. . ."[14] she writes.

In her lectures, she speaks directly to the "superwomen," on the fast track, into the "male race-with-success," and now the prime candidates for the heart attacks and lung diseases. She tells them over and over that they cannot be "Superwoman at the workplace and Supermom at home," that they must learn to give up "some of the power they normally wield at home to the New Man."

She worries about the women in the workplace, now successful and disillusioned, "hating" their confinement to rigid schedules, but unable to retreat. They are trapped by success and their new lifestyles.

She worries about women losing their traditional,

nurturing, caring qualities — as in her story of a "superwoman" lying ill and alone, and a so-called friend refusing to take the time to pick up her carton of milk.

She expresses the deepest regret at the Women's Liberation Movement's repudiation of volunteerism, that drove millions of women in the United States and Canada to resign from their beloved organizations, such as the IODE, Women's Institute, Big Sisters, and church auxiliaries. Innumerable communities would deteriorate with the loss of their caring services.

"NOW's infamous 1971 resolution on volunteerism," of which she did not approve, urged women to volunteer for social change and feminist groups, and not "in community service where their labour was exploited."[15] Betty Friedan entreats women to go back to volunteerism. "You shouldn't have to pay for, get paid for, passionate political effort to advance your own rights, or the well-being of the weak, or the noble cause of justice, art truth, community, nation, or of God," she writes.

She agonizes over the problems of single, unskilled mothers on welfare, and the single mothers with employable skills, but little supporting day care. She writes about the increases in female-headed households, a 46 per cent increase between 1970 and 1979.

In her lectures and books she describes the terrible, debilitating loneliness of the divorced, including her own. How she dreaded holidays "without a big enough family for gaiety."[16]

In *The Second Stage* and in her hour-and-a-half Florida lectures dealing with "The New Family," she is still attempting to paint the apparent demise of "the old family" as an evolutionary process, rather than the revolutionary historical development that it is now acknowledged to be. She reiterates her original thesis, that "the old family" to many a woman, determined "to move and earn and act in man's world...became her Frankenstein monster."[17]

Secular religion

However, she insists that the "old nuclear family" that formerly met "our needs of nurture, love and support," must be replaced by some other grouping as "all of us still have those needs."[18] She told us of a non-hippie country-house commune she had founded years ago, with friends, all in a similar "state of non-marriage," some with children, a grouping that supplied all the warmth and caring one might expect from any family. That it did not last she attributed to physical convenience factors. A man stood up in that lecture and asked her if the Israeli kibbutz was then a proper model, but she replied that it certainly was not, because women in the kibbutz were relegated to all the traditionally female jobs, such as child care, and were not treated as equal to the men in the army, being forbidden specific combat roles. (Equality means women beside men in the front lines, she still believes, although it seemed that all the women in the United States protested when President Carter adopted her theory, and presented a bill that would have conscripted young women as well as young men in the draft.)

Athough she hopes, prays, and talks incessantly about her "new groupings," she must surely know that in hundreds of surveys, few of them have been found to be working or credible. At the same time, new, powerful forces beginning to sweep across the United States may restore the traditional American family to supply again the "nurture, love and support" that we all need, that we all yearn for, that make life worth living. The Miss Teen Canada contestants may have given birth to such forces here in Canada.

We may still be capable of defeating the pessimism that emanates from our world-famous think tanks, such as The Hudson Institute, with its prediction that "the family and community may be replaced by impersonal, meritocratic organizations, filled with increasingly specialized technocrats and bourgeois bureaucrats."[19] (If we don't rise up to save them, I'm convinced this may happen.)

vs

new 'families'

Betty Friedan begs us to turn "a new corner — to transcend the present polarization between women and men, and between *women and women.*"[20] I believe this means that she is now ready to allow all women their own individual opinions, their own ideologies, their own choices, their own lifestyles, retiring the overpowering rhetoric that would still anchor their lives to the narrowing concepts of the Women's Liberation Movement.

In a lengthy interview, arranged by a Dean of the University of Florida in the spring of 1985, I came to see Betty Friedan as a victim as well as the originator of the feminist revolution. There were so many times she might have truthfully said: "That's not what we meant, not at all."

EPILOGUE

Are Canadians willing to accept a matriarchy? Are they resigned to all the ramifications of the Women's Liberation Movement that developed into a revolution of gigantic proportions, affecting the lives of every man, woman, and child on our continent? Primarily, are they happy that men and women generally have become separated, seeking their own individual goals, and marching to their own drums?

Maureen McTeer, in her *Chatelaine* column of February 1987, wrote: "According to preliminary federal estimates, by the year 2000, one in three women will never marry or will lose their spouse through separation, divorce or death."[1] Will we learn that the "Freedom of being single can be a brave new world?"[2] Are we ready for the loneliness?

Are we willing to listen to the death-knell of our traditional family? Hans Mohr, a sociologist and president of the revered Vanier Institute, the legacy of a great Canadian family, told *The Toronto Star* columnist Frank Jones that "the traditional family is dead. We are wasting our time [concerning ourselves with it]."[3] Yet the Institute's mandate was "the strengthening of family life." Now executives of the Institute stress the need for "familial" qualities in society.[4] Will they tell us where to look for those qualities? Where we can find the security and enveloping comfort we used to expect in a family?

Will we continue to turn our backs on the yearnings of many of our children for a mother *and* a father and anchors through their formative years? Will "a child without a father" continue to be accepted as a "norm" in our culture, or is it possible that Canadians may be educated to understand the need of most children for two parents? In an article entitled, "The Voice of Youth," appearing in the *Toronto Star* in February 1987, one 25-year-old Quebec woman said: "Sometimes I think it would be nice to have a child and not bother with a husband."[5]

In Britain there is a rapidly growing Families Need Fathers Group, and there is a European Men's Movement with 20,000 militant fathers demanding recognition and rights.[6] In the January 5, 1987 issue of *Time*, New York Senator Daniel P. Moynihan wrote: "A community that allows a large number of young men to grow up in broken families, dominated by women, never acquiring any stable relationship to male authority, never acquiring any set of rational expectations about the future — that community asks for and gets chaos. That is what we got: chaos."[7]

I am wondering if it is possible to bring all men back into favour by explaining that they never deserved the feminist image of them as the "evil oppressors," and "male chauvinist pigs." Furthermore, could women help them overcome an unjustified guilt complex?

Is it possible that somehow we may help to restore respect for the housewife-mother, acknowledging her inestimable contribution to our society? Would some other two-parent mothers consider leaving the workplace for the home front, if they are not able to secure the support of relatives or licensed day care for their children? Surely, then, governments would work out selective systems, finding the money for day care for the needful and single mothers (not the universal day care that surveys often have shown many women do not want).[8]

Would feminists ever again agree to be stereotyped as "unselfish,"[9] often allowing other considerations to take precedence over their "self-fulfillment"? This would never again signify a yoke, but simply a choice. Should we eliminate some of the "liberation" from the Women's Liberation Movement, realizing that some rules and restraints may be able to make our lives easier and our progress more orderly?

Must we continue to refuel our revolution with the fading voices of the American Women's Liberation Movement? In February 1986, Gloria Steinem, co-founder and editor of Ms., spoke to 800 Canadians attending the first annual Barbara Betcherman Memorial Fund Lecture in Osgoode Hall Law School in Toronto. She urged feminists to increase their "subversive" actions.

Will the time come when Canadian women wish to ignore such feminists and return to the mainstream? Then, will they agree to have Parliament and governments at every level in every province begin to dismantle the hundreds of Women's Councils and stop funding the thousands of women-coddling programs? No such astronomical funding has ever been considered in Britain or the United States and may be the answer to their more evolutionary accommodation of women's sudden, newly struck attitudes and aspirations of the Sixties and the Seventies. In Canada, with the cessation of funding, billions of dollars would sift back into federal, provincial, and municipal coffers, easing taxation, and aiding the deficit.

Have we reached a crossroads? Will we accept the matriarchy? Or will Canadian women now call a halt to the Women's Liberation Movement, and disarm? We could begin to clear away the debris after the fallout, and recognize and care for our wounded.

REFERENCES AND FURTHER READING

INTRODUCTION

1. George Gallup III, Empire Club Speech, March 7, 1985.
2. Herbert Marcuse, "Charles Reich as Revolutionary Ostrich" *The Con III Controversy: The Critics Look at* The Greening of America, Philip Nobile ed. (Pocket Books, Simon & Schuster, Inc., New York, 1971), p. 17.
3. Peter Marin, "Whispers of Uneasiness," *Ibid*, p. 31.
4. Nancy R. McWilliams, "Reich and Women," *Ibid*, p. 218.
5. Margaret Mead, *Aspects of the Present* (William Morrow and Co., in conjunction with *Redbook*, 1980).
6. Roland Barthes, *Mythologies* (Jonathan Cape Ltd., London, 1972).
7. Simone de Beauvoir, *The Second Sex* (Alfred A. Knopf, New York, 1953).
8. Stephen Strauss, "Pamphlet on sexual assumptions of researchers falls into own trap," *The Globe and Mail*, May 6, 1985.
9. C.G. Jung, *The Undiscovered Self* (Little, Brown and Co., Boston, 1957).

CHAPTER 1

1. *The Toronto Star,* July 3, 1985.
2. *The Globe and Mail,* July 7, 1985.
3. *Canadian Press,* July 5, 1985.
4. *The Financial Post,* December 15, 1984.
5. *The Globe and Mail,* April 9, 1985.
6. *The Bank of Montreal Quarterly,* January 31, 1985.

FURTHER READING

Statistics Canada Economic Reports, 1984, 1985.
United States Chamber of Commerce Reports, 1984, 1985.

CHAPTER 2

1. Betty Friedan, *The Second Stage* (Summit Books, New York, 1981), pp. 47-49.
2. Naomi Wall, "The Last Ten Years," in *Still Ain't Satisfied,* Maureen Fitzgerald, Connie Guberman, Margie Wolfe eds. (The Women's Press, Toronto, 1982), pp. 16, 17.
3. Betty Friedan, *Ibid.* , pp. 47-49.
4. Elaine Dewar, *Weekend Magazine,* April 2, 1977.
5. *The Globe and Mail,* March 27, 1984.
6. Shulamith Firestone, *The Dialectic of Sex* (William Morrow and Company, Inc., New York, 1970), p. 270.
7. *Weekend Magazine,* April 2, 1977.
8. *Maclean's Magazine,* March, 1970, pp. 38-42.
9. Susan Sontag, *Partisan Review,* Spring, 1973, p. 206.
10. *Chatelaine,* February, 1985, pp. 102, 106.
11. The Globe and Mail, July 6, 1985, p. 18.
12. *The Toronto Star,* August 24, 1985, p. M5.
13. *Psychology Today,* April, 1985, pp. 56-61.
14. *CBC Radio Noon Show,* Host, David Shatsky, November 14, 1985.

15. Patricia Hughes, "Fighting the Good Fight: Separation or Integration? in *Feminism in Canada: From Pressure to Politics,* Angela R. Miles and Geraldine Finn eds. (Black Rose Books, Montreal, 1982), p. 294.

FURTHER READING

C.T., "The Furious Feminist: Finding the Line Between Blame and Responsibility," *Ms.* , February, 1983, p. 81.

CHAPTER 3

1. *The Cambridge Ancient History,* Volume 2, J.B. Bury, S.A. Cook, F.E. Adcock eds. (The Cambridge University Press, Cambridge, England, 1924).

Judith Ochshorn, "The Contest between Androgyny and Patriarchy," *Feminist Visions,* Diane L. Fowlkes and Charlotte S. McLure eds. (University of Alabama Press, 1984), pp. 74-83.

Epochs of Ancient History, Epochs of Modern History, 27 Volumes, George W. Cox, Charles Sankey eds. (Charles Scribner's Sons, New York, 1889).

2. *Ibid.*

Columbia Encyclopaedia (Columbia University Press, New York, 1945), p. 1559.

3. *Ibid.*, p. 882.

Sally Alexander, "Women's Work in Nineteenth-Century London: A Study of the Years 1820-1850," *The Rights and Wrongs of Women,* Juliet Mitchell and Ann Oakley eds. (Penguin Books, Middlesex, England, 1976), pp. 59-111.

4. *Encyclopedia Britannica,* Volume 20 (1962), p. 437.

5. Margaret Walters, "The Rights and Wrongs of Women: Mary Wollstonecraft, Harriet Martineau, Simone de Beauvoir," *The Rights and Wrongs of Women,* p. 352.

6. *Ibid.*, p. 312.

Jane Flanders, "The Fallen Women in Fiction," *Feminist Visions,* p. 101.

Edna Nixon, *Mary Wollstonecraft, Her Life and Times* (Dent, London, 1971).

7. Eleanor Flexner, *Century of Struggle, The Women's Rights Movement in the United States* (Revised Edition, Belknap Press of Harvard University Press, Cambridge, Mass., 1975), pp. 46-51.
Catharine H. Burney, *Grimké Sisters, Sarah and Angelina Grimké* (Boston, Lee and Shepard, 1885; republished, Scholarly Press, St. Clair Shores, Michigan, 1970).

8. *The New General Encyclopaedia,* Ellsworth D. Foster, James Laughlin Hughes, Karl H. Goodwin eds. (General Press Service, Toronto, 1938), p. 3905.
E.C. Stanton, 1815-1902, Letters, Diaries, Theodore Stanton and Harriet Stanton Blatch eds. (Harper, New York, 1922).
Alma Lutz, *Created Equal: The Biography of Elizabeth Cady Stanton* (John Day, New York, 1940).

9. *Ibid.*

10. Anna Gordon, *The Beautiful Life of Frances E. Willard* (Women's Temperance Publishing Association, Chicago, 1898).

11. Katherine Anthony, *Susan B. Anthony: Her Personal History and Her Era* (Doubleday, New York, 1954).

12. Deborah Gorham, "The Canadian Suffragists," *Women in the Canadian Mosaic,* Gwen Matheson ed. (Peter Martin Associates, Toronto, 1976). pp. 35-42.

13. Nellie McClung, *The Stream Runs Fast* (T. Allen, Toronto, 1945), p. 27.

14. E. Sylvia Pankhurst, *The Suffragette Movement* (Longmans, Green and Company, London, 1981).
Encyclopaedia Britannica, Vol. 23 (1962), p. 711.

15. *Ibid.,* p. 708.

FURTHER READING

Andrew Sinclair, *The Better Half* (Harper and Row, New York, 1965).

Elizabeth Janeway, *Cross Sections* (William Morrow and Company Inc., New York, 1982).

William Chafe, *The American Woman: Her Changing Social, Economic, and Political Roles, 1920-1970* (Oxford University Press, 1972).

CHAPTER 4

1. Betty Friedan, *It Changed My Life* (Random House, Inc., New York, 1976), pp. xiii, xiv.
2. Betty Friedan, *The Feminine Mystique* (Dell Publishing Co., Inc., New York, 1963), pp. 292, 294, 295.
3. Janet Scott Barlow, "Motherhood and the Women's Movement," *Commonweal*, September 23, 1983, pp. 489-491
4. Barbara Grizzuti Harrison, "What Do Women Want?", *Harper's*, October, 1981, p. 39.
5. Lois Sweet, "Parents, Teachers Don't See Eye to Eye on PD Days," *The Toronto Star*, October 14, 1985.
6. C.G. Jung, *The Undiscovered Self*, R.F.C. Hull trans. (Little, Brown and Co., Boston, Toronto, 1957), p. 60.
7. Angela R. Miles, "Ideological Hegemony in Political Discourse," *Feminism in Canada: From Pressure to Politics*, Angela R. Miles and Geraldine Finn eds. (Black Rose Books, Montreal, 1982), p. 213.
8. *Ibid.*, Angela R. Miles, "Introduction," pp. 12, 13.
9. *Ibid.*, Geraldine Finn, "On the Oppression of Women in Philosophy," p. 301.
10. *Ibid.*, p. 303.
11. *Ibid.*, Mary O'Brien, "Feminist Praxis," "Feminism and Revolution," p. 253.
12. *Ibid.*, Mary O'Brien, "Feminist Theory and Feminist Practice," p. 261.
13. Mary O'Brien, *The Politics of Reproduction* (Routledge and Kegan Paul, London, 1981), reviewed by Angela Miles in *Canadian Women's Studies*, Volume 3, Number 4, pp. 63, 64.
14. Patricia Hughes, "Fighting the Good Fight: Separation or Integration?", *Feminism in Canada*, pp. 283, 284.
15. *Ibid.*, p. 286.
16. Dr. George Gelded, *Sexual Terrorism*, quoted in *Ms.*, April 8, 1983, p. 49.
17. Doris Anderson, "Women are Choosing to Go it Alone as Mothers," *The Toronto Star*, October 19, 1985.
18. Patricia Hughes, *Feminism in Canada, supra*, pp. 284, 286.
19. Jack Miller, "Scientists try to create life without males," *The Sunday Star*, Toronto, April 21, 1985.

20. Evans S. Novak, "Eleanor Smeal: Housewife who heads feminist group wants women to 'raise hell,'" *Star*, Tarrytown, New York, September 3, 1985, p. 35.

21. Lorne Slotnick, "Lesbian wants household called a family for benefits," and "Lesbian wins part inclusion of 'family' in benefits plan," *The Globe & Mail*, September 24, October 30, 1986.

22. *The Globe and Mail*, August 14, 1985.

23. Roland Barthes, *Mythologies* (Jonathan Cape Ltd., London, 1972), pp. 50, 51.

24. Rochelle Chadakoff, "Ms. Gloria Steinem essays everyday rebellions," *US*, October 24, 1983, pp. 38-40.

FURTHER READING

Rhona Rapoport, Robert Rapoport, *Dual-Career Families Re-examined: New Integrations of Work and Family* (Harper and Row, New York, 1976).

B. Ehrenreich, "A Feminist's View of the New Man," *New York Times Magazine*, May 20, 1984.

B. Abzug and M. Kelber, "How to win with the gender gap: 3 scenarios for the '84 elections," *Ms.*, March, 1984.

CHAPTER 5

1. Juliet Mitchell, *Woman's Estate* (Penguin Books, England, 1971), p. 127, quoting *The Daily Herald*, July 23, 1964.

2. *The Globe and Mail*, January 2, 1986.
The Toronto Star, July 31, 1985.
Chatelaine, July, 1984.

3. *Business Quarterly, Imperial Life Assurance Company of Canada Supplement*, Spring, 1984, p. 34.

4. *Chatelaine*, September, 1985, p. 46.
Business Quarterly, Imperial Life Assurance Company of Canada Supplement, Ibid, pp. 4-6.
Report on the Nation, November, 1984, pp. 77.

5. *The Globe and Mail*, March 22, 1985, p. 1.

6. *Ibid.*, June 21, 1985.
   The Toronto Star, May 30, 1984.
   Rick Byrne, Educational Director, CLC.
   Still Ain't Satisfied, Maureen Fitzgerald, Connie Guberman, Margie Wolfe eds. (The Women's Press, 1982), pp. 156-160.
7. *The Toronto Star*, February 7, 1986, p. B4.
8. *The Globe and Mail*, January 2, 1986.
9. *Still Ain't Satisfied*, pp. 141-151.
10. *Ibid.*
11. *Ibid.*, p. 134.
12. *The Globe and Mail*, February 11, 1986.
13. *The Toronto Star*, April 13, 1985.
14. *Ibid.*, March 8, 1986.
15. *Still Ain't Satisfied*, pp. 183-185.
16. *Report on Business Magazine*, December, 1985, p. 111.
17. *The Globe and Mail*, April 9, 1985.
18. *The Toronto Star*, September 13, 1985, p. B1.
19. *The Financial Post*, December 22, 1984.
20. *The Toronto Star*, October 22, 1984.
21. *The Globe and Mail*, November 28, 1985.
22. *Business Quarterly, Imperial Life Assurance Company of Canada Supplement, Ibid.*, pp. 6, 7.
23. *The Financial Post*, March 16, 1985.
24. *Maclean's*, October 1, 1984.
    Report on Business Magazine, November, 1985.
25. *The Financial Post Magazine*, December 1, 1985, pp. 27-32.
26. *Glamour*, February, 1986.
27. *Today Morning Television Show*, March 20, 1986.
28. *The Toronto Star*, February 13, 1986.

FURTHER READING

Publications: Women's Bureau, United States Department of Labor, Washington, D.C.

Publications: National Organization for Women, 509 Fifth Avenue, New York.

Edmund Dahlstrom, *The Changing Roles of Men and Women* (Beacon Press, Boston, 1971).

Face to Face: Fathers, Mothers, Masters, Monsters — Essays for a Non-Sexist Future, Meg McGavran Murray ed. (Greenwood Press, Westport, Connecticut, 1983).

S. Gordon, "The New Corporate Feminism," *Nation*, February 3, 1983.

J. Kagan, "Work in the 1980's and 1990's," *Working Woman*, April, 1983.

"Latest on Unisex Job Movement" (Census Bureau Statistics), United States, *U.S. News World*, May 9, 1983.

W.F. Buckley, "Welcome to a Man's World," *Vogue*, August, 1983.

CHAPTER 6

1. Friedrich Engels, *The Origin of the Family, Private Property and the State*, (International Publishers, New York, 1942), p. 152.
2. V. I. Lenin, *The Tasks of the Proletariat in our Revolution, 1917* (Lawrence Publishing, London, 1932), p. 121.
3. *The Globe and Mail*, February 27, 1986.
4. Michael Wilson, CBC, February 26, 1986.
5. *The Globe and Mail*, March 5, 1986.
6. *Ibid.*
7. Donald Johnson, Liberal Leadership candidacy address.
8. *The Toronto Star*, August 12, 1985.
9. *Chatelaine*, September, 1985, p. 46.
10. *The Globe and Mail*, December 2, 1985, p. A19.
11. *Canadian Press*, October 27, 1984.
12. *The Toronto Star*, February 2, 1986.
13. *Ibid.*
14. *The Globe and Mail*, October 17, 1985, p. A24.
15. *Ibid.*
16. *Ibid.*
17. *Chatelaine*, April, 1985, p. 36.
18. *The Toronto Star*, October 16, 1985, p. A9.
19. *Ibid.*
20. *Chatelaine*, August, 1985, p. 28.
21. *Working Woman*, October, 1985, p. 118.

22. *Vital Speeches of the Day*, April 1, 1985, pp. 382-384.
23. *The Toronto Star*, February 12, 13, 1986.
24. *Newsweek*, April 22, 1985.
25. *Influence*, December/January, 1986.
26. *Report on Business*, December, 1985, p. 112.
27. *Maclean's*, October 1, 1984.
28. *The Toronto Star*, October 18, 1984.
29. *The Globe and Mail*, November 20, 1985.
30. *Working Woman*, October, 1985, p. 118.
    Newsweek, April 22, 1985, p. 57.
31. *Maclean's*, April 16, 1984, p. 46.
32. *Vital Speeches of the Day*, April 1, 1985, p. 383.
33. *Newsweek*, April 22, 1985, p. 57.
34. Janet Radcliffe Richards, *The Skeptical Feminist* (Routledge & Kegan Paul, London, Boston, Henley, 1980), pp. 116, 117.
35. *The Toronto Star*, November 20, 23, 1985; August 5, 1985, p. A9; February 11, 1986.
    Chatelaine, September, 1984.
36. *The Toronto Star*, February 16, 1986, p. H4.
37. *The Globe and Mail*, February 25, 1986.
    The Toronto Star, February 25, 1986.

FURTHER READING

Leo Kanowitz, *Women and The Law: The Unfinished Revolution* (University of New Mexico Press, Albuquerque, 1969).

S. Gordon, "The New Corporate Feminism," *Nation*, February 3, 1983, p. 129.

J. Kagan, "Work in the 1980's and 1990's," *Work Woman*, April, 1983, p. 26.

W.F. Buckley, "Welcome to a Man's World," *Vogue*, August, 1983.

"Latest on Unisex Job Movement" (Census Bureau Statistics), *U.S. News World*, May 9, 1983.

Edmund Dahlstrom, *The Changing Roles of Men and Women* (Beacon Press, Boston, 1971).

Caroline Hennessey, *The Strategy of Sexual Struggle* (Lancer Books, New York, 1971).

Studs Terkel, *Working* (Avon, New York, 1975).

Midge Decter, "Liberating Women: Who Benefits?", *Commentary*, March, 1984. "Judges have shown themselves to be particularly susceptible to all the items on a rapidly expanding roster of fashionable social theories, and they, in turn, have succeeded in convincing many employers of the costly but convenient virtues of compliance with their findings. But husbands, teachers, colleagues, and classmates?" (p. 31).

CHAPTER 7

1. Margaret Atwood, *Life Before Man* (Seal Books, Toronto, 1979).
2. Ira Wood, *The Kitchen Man* (The Crossing Press, New York, 1986).
3. Jane Rule, *A Hot-Eyed Moderate* (Lester & Orpen Dennys Ltd., Toronto, 1986).
4. *The Toronto Star*, April 20, 1986.
5. C.G. Jung, *The Undiscovered Self* (Little, Brown and Co., Boston, 1957), pp. 71, 72.
6. Carolyn G. Heilbrun, *Reinventing Womanhood* (W.W. Norton & Company, New York, 1979).
7. *The Toronto Star*, July 4, 1984.
8. *Maclean's*, April 15, 1985.
9. *Ibid.*, April 28, 1986.
10. *Time*, January 28, 1985.
11. *Flare*, February, 1985.
12. *The Toronto Star*, August 28, 1985.
13. *The Globe and Mail*, April 18, 1985.
14. Shulamith Firestone, *The Dialectic of Sex* (William Morrow and Company, Inc., New York, 1970), pp. 71, 72, 255, 272, 273.
15. *The Toronto Star*, February 7, 1986.
16. *Ibid.*, July 16, 1986.
17. *The Toronto Sun*, July 16, 1986.
18. *McCall's*, July, 1985, p. 73.
19. *The Toronto Star*, January 26, 1985.

20. *Ibid.*, March 17, 1985.
21. *Ibid.*, June 21, 1985.
22. *The Globe and Mail*, November 1, 1985.
23. *Ibid.*, April 17, 1985.
24. *Ibid.*, September 25, 1985.
25. *The Toronto Star*, October 18, 1984.
26. *Ibid.*, November 8, 1985.
27. *Ibid.*, May 3, 1986.
28. *The Globe and Mail*, February 5, 1985.
29. Margaret Mead, *Aspects of the Present* (William Morrow and Company, Inc., 1980, in conjunction with *Redbook*), p. 103.

FURTHER READING

Suzanne Gordon, "The New Corporate Feminism," *The Nation*, February 5, 1983, p. 143.

Mona Charen, "The Feminist Mistake," *National Review*, March 23, 1984.

M. Decter, "Liberating Women: who benefits?", *Commentary*, March, 1984.

"Have Men Changed? 19 Women's Views," "Fatherhood Yesterday," *U.S. News & World Report*, June 3, 1985.

Janet Radcliffe Richards, *The Skeptical Feminist* (Routledge & Kegan Paul, London, Boston, Henley, 1980).

Linda K. Kerber, Jane De Hart Matthews, *Women's America* (Oxford University Press, New York, 1982).

Vance Packard, *The Sexual Wilderness: The Contemporary Upheaval in Male-Female Relationships* (David McKay Co., New York, 1968).

Charles Winick, *The New People: Desexualization in American Life* (Pegasus, New York, 1968).

Jane Adams, "Catch-35," *Working Woman*, September, 1983, pp. 140ff.

P. Clayton, "Professional women, suicide, and depression," *USA Today*, April, 1983.

H. Goldberg, "The Female Forecast: Who will you be in 10 years?", *Mademoiselle*, May, 1984.

M. Clements, "Terminal Cool," *Esquire*, March, 1984.

CHAPTER 8

1. *The Globe and Mail*, April 29, 1986.
2. *The Toronto Star*, August 28, 1985.
3. *Ibid*, March 8, 1986.
4. *Maclean's*, May 20, 1985.
5. *Ibid*.
6. *Fortune*, April 14, 1986.
   Sarasota Herald Tribune, January 27, 1986.
   Senator Daniel Patrick Moynihan, *Family and Nation* (Harcourt, Brace, Jovanovich, San Diego, California, 1986).
7. *Newsweek*, July 15, 1985.
8. *The Globe and Mail*, May 5, 1983.
9. *The Toronto Star*, April 7, 1986.
10. *The Globe and Mail*, May 5, 1983.
11. *Sarasota Herald Tribune*, February 1, 1986.
12. *Town and Country*, June, 1982.
13. *Chatelaine*, April, 1986.
14. Alvin Toffler, *Future Shock* (Bantam Books, New York, 1971), p. 252. The author who described the former (traditional) family as the "giant shock absorber" of society, discussed at length "The Fractured Family" and "The Limits of Adaptability."
15. *The Toronto Star*, February 7, 1986.
16. *Ibid.*, August 13, 1985.
17. Canadian Press, August 12, 1985.
18. *The Toronto Star*, August 12, 1985.
19. *Sarasota Herald Tribune*, February 1, 1986.
20. *The Toronto Star*, August 12, 1985.
21. *Ibid.*, May 3, 1985.
22. *Ibid.*
23. *Ibid.*
24. *The Plain Truth*, April, 1985.
25. *The Toronto Star*, November 9, 1985.
26. *Ibid.*, February 12, 1986.
27. *Ibid.*
28. *Rotary Voice*, September 28, 1984.
    Donahue Show, CBS T.V., January 30, 1986.
29. *The Toronto Star*, April 21, 1985.

30. Nancy Chodorow, *The Reproduction of Mothering: Psychoanalysis and the Sociology of Gender* (University of California Press, Berkeley, 1978).
    Mona Charen, "The Feminist Mistake," *National Review,* March 23, 1984, pp. 24-27. "Perhaps my grandchildren will look back on our era as socially aberrant ('Did they really want boys and girls to be the same, Grandma?') Perhaps not. One thing is certain. It's up to the women. Organized booing or not, women transmit culture. If feminist competitiveness loses, feminine contentment will win" (p. 27).
31. *The Globe and Mail*, March 6, 1986.
32. Public Relations Department, University of Toronto.
33. *The Toronto Star*, June 27, 1985.
34. *The Globe and Mail*, April 24, 1986.

FURTHER READING

Nancy R. McWilliams, "Reich and Women," in *The Con III Controversy: The Critics Look at* The Greening of America (Pocket Books, Simon & Schuster, Inc., New York, 1971): "The one thing we surely know about what makes kids strong and whole — 'together' in Reich's language — is that they need security, stability, and comprehensibility while growing up.... The loss of the extended family and the stable community has left women lonely and frustrated, their lives empty, and the health of their children dangerously vulnerable to their mothers' mood swings..." (p. 219).

CHAPTER 9

1. *The Toronto Star*, April 4, 1985.
2. *Ibid.*, March 5, 1985.
3. *Weekend Magazine*, September 30, 1978, p. 10.
4. *Ibid.*, p. 16.
5. *Ibid.*
6. *Ibid.*
7. *The Toronto Star*, March 10, 1985.

8. *Council Update*, Newsletter, Ontario Advisory Council on Women's Issues, January, 1985, p. 4.
9. *Chatelaine*, editorial, June, 1985.
10. *The Toronto Star*, March 30, 1985.
11. Lena Beryl Associates Survey, May-October, 1985.
12. *The Toronto Star*, March 10, 1985.
13. *The Sunday Sun*, Toronto, August 19, 1984.
14. *Ibid.*
15. *Ibid.*
16. Veronica Strong-Boag, Introduction to *In Times Like These*, by Nellie McClung (University of Toronto Press, Toronto, 1972), p. xix.
17. *The Toronto Star*, March 1, 1985.
18. *Maclean's*, August 29, 1983.
19. *Ibid.*
20. *The Toronto Star*, March 25, 1985.
21. *The Globe and Mail*, March 27, 1985.
22. *Ibid.*, August 20, 1984.
23. *Chatelaine*, December, 1984, p. 142.
24. Seminar, University of Florida, Sarasota Campus, February, 1985.
25. *Weekend Magazine*, September 30, 1978.
26. *Maclean's*, February 27, April 16, 1984.
27. Geraldine Finn, "Questions of Appearance," *Canadian Forum*, August-September, 1984, pp. 45-47.
    The Toronto Sun, April 2, 1985.
    The Globe and Mail, April 2, 1985.

CHAPTER 10

1. Betty Friedan, *It Changed My Life* (Random House, Inc., New York, 1976), p. xiv.
2. *Ibid.*, p. xix
3. *Ibid.*, p. 34.
4. *Ibid.*, p. 18.
5. *Ibid.*, p. 30.

6. Betty Friedan, *The Second Stage* (Summit Books, Simon & Schuster, New York, 1981), p. 46.
7. *Ibid.*, p. 47.
8. Marilyn French, "The Emancipation of Betty Friedan," *Esquire*, December, 1983, pp. 510-517.
9. *The Second Stage*, p. 138.
10. *Ibid.*, p. 137.
11. *Ibid.*, p. 38.
12. *Ibid.*, p. 38.
13. *Ibid.*, p. 157.
14. *Ibid.*, p. 15.
15. *Ibid.*, p. 333.
16. *It Changed My Life*, p. 194.
17. *The Second Stage*, p. 93.
18. *Ibid.*, p. 53.
19. Robert S. Pickett, "Tomorrow's Family," *Intellect*, April, 1977, p. 331.
20. *The Second Stage*, p. 41.

FURTHER READING

"Have Men Changed? 19 Women's Views," *U. S. News & World Report*, June 3, 1985.

Marjorie Schaevitz, "The Superwoman Syndrome," *USA Today*, December, 1983.

EPILOGUE

1. *Chatelaine*, February, 1987, p. 44.
2. *The Toronto Star*, September 16, 1986.
3. *Ibid.*, April 18, 1984.
4. *Ibid.*, April 19, 1984.
5. *Ibid.*, February 22, 1987.
6. *Ibid.*, April 19, 1984.
7. *Time*, January 5, 1987.
8. *The Globe and Mail*, April 29, 1986.
9. *The Feminist Takeover*, Chapter VII.

The following publishers have generously given permission to reprint material from copyrighted works: Routledge and Kegan Paul, from *The Sceptical Feminist* by Janet Radcliffe Richards (1980), and from *The Politics of Reproduction* by Mary O'Brien (1981). Reprinted by permission of Routledge and Kegan Paul. Simon and Schuster, Inc., from *The Con III Controversy: The Critics Look at* The Greening of America, Philip Nobile, ed. (1971). Reprinted by permission of Simon and Schuster, Inc. From *Feminism in Canada: From Pressure to Politics.* Reprinted with the kind permission of BLACK ROSE BOOKS, Montreal, *Feminism in Canada: From Pressure to Politics,* A. R. Miles and G. Finn, eds., 1982. The Toronto Star Syndicate, from Lois Sweet's article, "Parents, Teachers Don't See Eye to Eye on PD Days" (appearing in *The Toronto Star,* October 14, 1985). Reprinted with permission — The Toronto Star Syndicate. The Women's Press, Toronto, from *Still Ain't Satisfied,* Maureen Fitzgerald, Connie Guberman, Margie Wolfe, eds. (1982). Reprinted by permission of the Women's Press, Toronto. Random House, Inc., from *It Changed My Life: Writings on the Women's Movement* by Betty Friedan (1976). Reprinted by permission of Random House, Inc. Commonweal Foundation, from "Motherhood and the Women's Movement," by Janet Scott Barlow (appearing in *Commonweal,* Sept. 23, 1983). Copyright © Commonweal Foundation. W. W. Norton Inc., from *The Feminine Mystique* by Betty Friedan. Copyright 1983, 1974, 1973, 1963, by Betty Friedan. Reprinted by permission of W.W. Norton Inc. Thanks are also due to Mr. George Gallup III of the Gallup Poll Organization, for permission to quote from his speech to the Empire Club, March 7, 1985, and to Doris Anderson, for permission to reprint material from her article "Women Are Choosing to Go It Alone As Mothers" (*The Toronto Star*, Oct. 19, 1985).